On These
PROMISING SHORES
of the PACIFIC

A History of Saint Mary's College

Ronald Eugene Isetti

Charleston · London

THE
History
PRESS

Published by The History Press
Charleston, SC 29403
www.historypress.net

Cover images courtesy of the Saint Mary's College Archives, Moraga, and the Office of
College Communications, with special thanks to Martin Cohen and Karen Kemp.

First published 2013

Manufactured in the United States

ISBN 978.1.62619.276.8

Library of Congress CIP data applied for.

For my nephew, Derek, whose talents continue to dazzle me.

Thanks for the memories, Carole!

Sally J.

Dec.
2013

Contents

Archival Abbreviations   7

Acknowledgements   9

1. An Archbishop's Dream: The Founding of Saint Mary's College, 1859–1868   11

2. Renewed Hope: The Arrival of the De La Salle Christian Brothers, 1868–1879   23

3. At the Crossroads: The Latin Question and Possible Eviction, 1868–1879   38

4. "The Athens of the Pacific": Saint Mary's College Moves to Oakland, 1879–1900   47

5. A Technical College: Saint Mary's College Changes Its Colors, 1900–1923   59

6. A Second Spring: Saint Mary's College Moves to Moraga, 1923–1928   73

7. The Golden Age: A Cathedral College in the European Tradition, 1928–1934   86

8. The College Declares Bankruptcy: The Presidency of Brother Albert Rahill, 1934–1941   99

9. Saint Mary's College in War and Peace: The Presidency of Brother Austin Crowley, 1941–1950   110

10. The Korean War Crisis: The Presidency of Brother Thomas Levi, 1950–1956   122

CONTENTS

11. Changing Times: The Presidencies of Brother Albert Plotz and
   Brother Michael Quinn, 1956–1969   131
12. Years of Turmoil, Years of Progress: The Presidency of Brother
   Mel Anderson, 1969–1997   145
13. A Promise Unfulfilled: The Presidency of Brother Craig Franz,
   1997–2005   162
14. A Time of Restoration: The Presidency of Brother Ronald Gallagher,
   2005–2013   174

Notes   187
Bibliography   201
Index   203
About the Author   208

Archival Abbreviations

AASF: Archives of the Archdiocese of San Francisco (Menlo Park)
ABLB: Archives of Bancroft Library (Berkeley)
ACBR: Archives of the Christian Brothers (Rome)
APGR: Archives of the Procurator General (Rome)
ASMC: Archives of Saint Mary's College (Moraga)
ASFD: Archives of the San Francisco District (Napa)
LSRL: Lasallian Research Library (Moraga)

Acknowledgements

I would like to thank the many archivists, friends and colleagues who offered me assistance and encouragement during the five-year period this history was researched and written. Let me start with the archivists. I am especially grateful to Andrea Miller of the Christian Brothers archives in Napa for finding and duplicating scores of documents for me, answering innumerable questions by e-mail and helping me find photos for this book. She also read an early manuscript and offered excellent suggestions for improvement. Cheerful, efficient and prompt, Andrea has been a pleasure to work with. I am also grateful to Martin Cohen and his student assistants at the Saint Mary's College archives in Moraga, namely, Melissa Campbell, Gabriel Ladd, Alexia Jarvis and Daniel Farrell. They all helped me search for documents and photos and kept the archives open beyond usual business hours for my convenience. Dr. Jeffrey Burns of the San Francisco Archdiocesan Archives was helpful in locating documents dealing with the early history of the college and its bankruptcy during the Great Depression. Finally, I want to thank Brother Francois Ricousse FSC, archivist at the Christian Brothers' generalate in Rome, for his assistance in pulling documents on the Latin Question and for putting up with my halting French.

Let me now turn to my readers. The following read all or part of various versions of the book and offered constructive criticism: Brother Raphael Patton, Brother Mel Anderson, Brother Craig Franz, Brother Kenneth Cardwell, my novitiate confrere Dr. David DePew, Dr. Robert Roxby, Dr. Thomas Slakey, Dr. Katherine Roper, Dr. Roy Wensley, Dr. Edward Porcella,

Dr. Carl Guarneri, Dr. Keith Brandt, Dr. Gretchen Lemke-Santangelo, Dr. Bethami "Beth" Dobkin, Dr. William Hynes, Gerald McKevitt SJ, Daniel Whitehurst and Randall Andrada. I give them credit for the good features of this history and assume responsibility for any errors I may have made. Last but not least, I want to thank Aubrie Koenig of The History Press for helping me at every point along the way to bring this book to birth. She is a professional in every sense of the word.

In writing this book, I have made extensive use of three earlier histories of Saint Mary's, and I want to gratefully and fully acknowledge my dependence on them. The first is a typed manuscript written by Brother Cyril Ashe in 1917. He was a careful amateur historian who used reliable sources. The second is a centennial history of Saint Mary's written by Brother Matthew McDevitt in 1963; it was later published privately in mimeograph form under the title of *The First Century of Saint Mary's College, 1863–1963*. A trained historian with a doctorate from the Catholic University, Brother Matthew makes use of Brother Cyril's earlier history and concentrates on the early years of Saint Mary's in San Francisco and Oakland. I have looked at almost all of the sources he unearthed. The third is the saga of the Galloping Gaels football team written by alumnus Randall Andrada under the title of *They Did It Every Time*. Although the work of an undergraduate, it is remarkably well written, jazzy and insightful. Much of the factual information taken from these three sources has not been endnoted because of severe space constraints, but direct quotations have all been properly cited. I have not cited material whose source is clearly indicated in the text.

Chapter 1

An Archbishop's Dream
·····························
The Founding of Saint Mary's College,
1859–1868

Saint Mary's College was the brainchild of the Most Reverend Joseph Sadoc Alemany, first archbishop of San Francisco. It was his educational vision that gave birth to the school and his caring oversight that sustained it during its fitful infancy. Joseph was born in the Catalonian city of Vich on July 13, 1814. He entered the Dominican friary of his hometown at sixteen, later fled from religious persecution in Spain and was ordained in Italy on March 11, 1837. Three years later, Friar Sadoc, the name he was given in religion, was sent to the American "missions," serving in Ohio, Kentucky and Tennessee as a parish priest, seminary president and provincial religious superior. In 1845, he became a proud American citizen.[1]

In the summer of 1850, the Holy See named Alemany to the Bishopric of Monterey in far-off California, until two years earlier a remote province of the Federal Republic of Mexico. After President James K. Polk provoked war with Mexico in 1846, the United States acquired vast new borderlands in the Southwest. The bishop's chair in Monterey had sat vacant since 1846, following the death of Mexican bishop Francisco Garcia Diego y Moreno of the Franciscan order. Before the American conquest, the Catholic Church in California was in almost complete disarray, its few priests mostly old or sick and its adobe church buildings falling apart. The once flourishing Franciscan missions had fallen into decay after being secularized in 1834.

Alemany resolved to refuse his daunting new assignment, but Pope Pius IX was adamant. In a letter to his mother, the young missionary reported that during a papal audience, the Supreme Pontiff had told him in perfect

Castilian: "You are to go to Monterey; you must go to California. Others go there to seek gold; you go there to carry the Cross."[2] Three years after Alemany took office, his see was divided, and he was transferred to San Francisco on July 29, 1853. To care for some sixty thousand Catholics, the newly appointed archbishop had at his disposal only twenty-two priests, scattered over some 260,000 square miles. Securing clergy to staff his churches and money to build them was Archbishop Alemany's most pressing priority. However, he was also determined to establish a Catholic school system in his ecclesiastical jurisdiction as quickly as possible.

In March 1851, the new archbishop installed two Italian Jesuits at the decrepit Franciscan mission of Santa Clara and authorized them to found a college on the premises. Four years later, he encouraged the Society of Jesus to erect Saint Ignatius College (now the University of San Francisco) on the south side of Market Street in San Francisco proper. However, the archbishop was disappointed with both institutions. In his estimation, only the wealthy could afford Santa

Clara's annual fees of $400. He vigorously protested, and the president reluctantly reduced them to $350.[3] Alemany was also upset by what he regarded as the high costs of St. Ignatius College. In an 1862 letter to Archbishop John Baptist Purcell of Cincinnati, he said that he had invited the Jesuit Fathers to open a college in San Francisco proper "with a view to have the Catholic boys of this city taught almost gratuitously" but that instead they "charged [their students] rather too much."[4] What is perhaps even more important, the Jesuits at both of their colleges were not producing sufficient candidates for the archdiocesan major seminary.

The archbishop therefore decided to proceed with plans to build a diocesan college to his

Archbishop Alemany, the founder of Saint Mary's College. *Courtesy of Christian Brothers Archives, Napa.*

own specifications. He had two major goals in mind: to foster vocations to the secular priesthood and to provide an affordable higher education for young Catholic men in the Far West. Alemany planned to charge only $150 a year in tuition and board for resident students. As a result, the Jesuit Fathers "looked to the future with anxiety, waiting to see what effect the founding of Saint Mary's…would have on Santa Clara's enrollment." In May 1863, cofounder Father Michael Accolti bitterly complained in a "Financial Report" that "the purpose of this new institution is ostensibly to put down Santa Clara." He fully expected that for two or three years the enrollment of his little mission college would suffer, as students "rushed" to Alemany's new diocesan school on account of its lower costs.[5]

Father James Croke Tramps the Mother Lode

In securing funds to build a college for "the children of Miners, Mechanics, and Agriculturists,"[6] Alemany enlisted the fundraising talents of Father James Croke. Ordained in Paris in 1850, Croke volunteered as a young priest for the missions of the Oregon Territory. Handsome and youthful, he made a favorable impression on all who met him. First landing in San Francisco in September 1850, en route to the Pacific Northwest, Father Croke remained in the city longer than expected to minister to the needs of a desperate local population recoiling from a cholera epidemic. Early in 1851, he finally made his way north to Oregon Territory, where he served for four years at various frontier posts. During his tenure in the Pacific Northwest, the young priest, in the company of a Jesuit missionary, rode on horseback across the Cascades and Rocky Mountains as far east as Fort Benton on the Missouri River. According to Brother Matthew McDevitt, "From the time he left the last white settlement, about 100 miles from Portland, until he reached his destination, some 1,800 miles, he met only nine white men, six Jesuits, two Canadian trappers and a half-breed scout."[7] This arduous journey through wild country accustomed Croke to the rugged life of the frontiersman and prepared him well for another long trek he would undertake a few years later that would figure prominently in the founding of Saint Mary's College.

In 1855, Father Croke applied for admission to the Archdiocese of San Francisco because the damp climate of Oregon was injurious to his health. Two years later, he was finally able to make the move. On October 11, 1859, Archbishop Alemany sent Croke on a barnstorming tour of Northern California

Father James Croke, who raised the money to build Saint Mary's. *Courtesy of Christian Brothers Archives, Napa.*

to raise funds for his projected new diocesan college. The intrepid young Irishman first sailed from San Francisco to Trinidad in Humboldt County, where he disembarked and began a grueling ride on horseback to backwoods settlements and remote diggings in far Northern California. His first stop was Sawyer's Bar, one hundred miles inland from the coast on the north fork of the Salmon River. The local parish priest, an Austrian Benedictine, made the first donation of twenty dollars to the new school.[8]

Father Croke eventually visited 224 towns, hamlets, mining camps, settlements and diggings from the Oregon border down to the Mother Lode, over to the Sacramento and San Joaquin Valleys and finally back to the San Francisco Bay Area. He made his way from place to place on foot and by horseback, snowshoe, riverboat and stagecoach. His trail togs paid homage both to the wild county through which he passed and to his religious calling as a Catholic priest—Croke's khaki-colored duster, which he wore on horseback, could be rapidly reversed into a black clerical soutane or cassock when he dismounted and walked through the streets of the many places he visited, soliciting funds and ministering to the spiritual needs of the faithful at the same time. After two years of hard work, Father Croke was able to hand over to a grateful archbishop more than $37,000 from 7,540 donors. This was enough money to begin construction but not to cover the total cost of building the new diocesan college, which eventually would climb to $150,000. To complete the project, actually only about half of it, Alemany would be forced to secure large loans, totaling $100,000, from the Hibernia Savings and Loan Bank in San Francisco. This indebtedness would later create serious financial problems for the new school and, in a few short years, bring it to the very brink of bankruptcy.

On the Old Mission Road to San Jose

Construction of the new campus began early in 1862 on a sixty-acre tract called University Mound and later College Hill; it was located four and a half miles to the south of the city proper on the Old Mission Road to San Jose. On July 25, 1853, Archbishop Alemany had acquired sixty acres from Jose Jesus and Carmen Sibrian de Bernal, prominent citizens of Mexican California, for the bargain basement price of only $1,600. The parcel had once formed part of the family's vast Rancho Rincon de las Salinas y Potrero Viejo. Old photographs of the institution reveal an isolated, even forlorn campus. Today, the original site of Saint Mary's College is situated between Bernal Heights and the Excelsior District in a bell-shaped neighborhood named Saint Mary's Park.

The erection of the college buildings sputtered because of a shortage of bricks. To remedy the problem, Alemany decided to erect a kiln on site and dig up the local clay; as a result, "the brick that went into the beautiful Gothic pile of old Saint Mary's College was burnt on the site."[9] By midsummer, sufficient progress had been made to set a date for laying the cornerstone on August 3, 1862. During an impressive ceremony, this Latin inscription was inserted into the granite cornerstone, anchoring the new school in space and time:

> *On the third day of the month of August, in the year of Our Lord 1862, in the sixteenth of the pontificate of Pope Pius IX, Abraham Lincoln being President*

A long-distance view of Saint Mary's College in San Francisco showing its isolation. *Courtesy of Christian Brothers Archives, Napa.*

of the United States of America, and Leland Stanford being Governor of the State of California, the illustrious and Most Reverend Joseph S. Alemany, O.S.D., Archbishop of California, laid the cornerstone of this college, under the title of St. Mary, for the instruction of the youth of California, not in literature merely, but what is greater, in true Christian knowledge. It has been erected by the offerings of the miners and the Faithful of California, through the exertions of the Very Rev. James Croke, Vicar General.[10]

In 1862, Langley's *San Francisco Directory* boasted that the college's location possessed "all the advantages of a salubrious situation, commanding an extensive view of the Bay and the surrounding scenery."[11] The view from Saint Mary's was indeed sweeping, but only when not obscured by the frequent fogs that enveloped the school. However, the site was hardly healthy. Exposed to the elements, the little college was often blasted by cold ocean winds that would rattle windows on stormy nights and drive younger students to their knees begging "for the chance to go to confession."[12] Although not blessed with a clement climate, Saint Mary's had plenty of room for growth. The little college would be set in the middle of a seven-acre campus, enclosed by a fence; the remaining fifty-three acres of surrounding school property consisted of cultivated farmland that would eventually supply the institution with all the milk, butter, vegetables and hay it might require.

The archbishop personally supervised the construction of the new college. His journals, account books and personal diary are filled with notations on how Saint Mary's was progressing from day to day. Attentive to the smallest detail, the archbishop recorded on March 13, 1863, that he had paid $9.25 for "horse feed" at Saint Mary's College, doubtless for the draft animals used in construction.[13] Alemany also busied himself with administrative matters such as setting the new college's tuition and fees. This, of course, was a vital matter for him. In a May 1863 letter to an inquirer, he noted that "$150 will be charged to each student for board and tuition etc. during the scholastic year of 11 months. This pension must be paid semiannually in advance."[14] Faculty appointments were turned over to Father John F. Harrington, a diocesan priest with considerable experience in Catholic elementary and secondary education.

It took approximately a year to build the new campus. The main academic building was an imposing Gothic edifice with pointed recessed arches, dormer windows and buttresses. The original plans of architect Thomas England called for a large main building and two wings forming a T; only one-half of the main academic building was completed, along with one of

An artist's depiction of Saint Mary's College in San Francisco, showing the chapel that was never built. *Courtesy of Christian Brothers Archives, Napa.*

the two projected wings, which was topped by a lantern tower. The chapel that is often pictured in pen-and-ink drawings of the first Saint Mary's College was never erected.

Alemany had finally decided to locate Saint Mary's College several miles from the city proper in order to protect the morals of its students. For a time, he had considered building his new school on a square block bounded by Larkin, Polk, Grove and Hayes Streets in the present downtown area of San Francisco. However, the archbishop eventually concluded that this parcel was too small for a college campus and too close to sinful allures of the Barbary Coast and Chinatown. In early 1861, Alemany even dickered with the local Methodists to purchase their Collegiate Institute in Napa (this school eventually merged in 1896 with the University of the Pacific, then located in San Jose) as a sufficiently safe and secluded location for his new institution of higher learning. Both sides settled on an acceptable price, but the sale was called off at the last minute when the deed to the property proved defective.

SAINT MARY'S COLLEGE OPENS ITS DOORS

In the middle of the bloody Civil War, on July 9, 1863, Archbishop Alemany officially dedicated his new diocesan college. With remarkable simplicity, he recorded the event in his daily journal: "I bless [today the] little chapel at Saint Mary's College beyond the Mission of Dolores..."[15] A few days earlier, General Meade had blunted General Lee's thrust into the North at Gettysburg, and General Grant had overpowered the Mississippi River port of Vicksburg in the Confederacy. Although far removed from searing scenes of combat and carnage, Saint Mary's still felt the touch of the Civil War. Shortly after classes opened in the summer of 1863, Federal draft officials moved onto campus to register all male residents between twenty and forty-five years old. More concerned with apprehending bounty jumpers and deserters than with conscripting young men into military service, they left when no suspicious characters were found and never returned.

Alemany had hoped to place his new college under the direction of a religious order devoted to teaching. However, when this was not possible, he staffed it with lay professors and diocesan priests. Most of the latter were not well suited to the work of Catholic higher education. The one notable exception was the first president, Father John F. Harrington. In 1859, Alemany named him principal of the secondary school he had established in 1855 in the basement of Saint Mary's Cathedral at California and Dupont Streets. In significant respects, this academy would serve as the nucleus for Saint Mary's College; its erstwhile principal would become the first president, and several faculty members would transfer

Father John Harrington, the first president of Saint Mary's College. *Courtesy of Christian Brothers Archives, Napa.*

to the new school when it opened in 1863. Both institutions also shared the same name. In its early years, Saint Mary's College, like its predecessor, was in many respects a glorified high school, placing heavy emphasis on the three R's and the fourth R of religion. Most of the students were enrolled in the preparatory and commercial departments, and only a few pursued advanced courses in the classics and science.

Father Cornelius Gallagher, an Irish immigrant and former pastor of Saint Rose's Church in Sacramento, was named the vice-president and placed in charge of non-academic departments. His appointment proved a major mistake. Although warmhearted, he could also be quarrelsome and stubborn. As a result, Alemany admonished Gallagher to work under "the direction of the 'Board'" and show "due respect to the President of the College."[16] Apparently, he did not heed this sound advice and was soon replaced.

The first enrollees at Saint Mary's ranged in age from baby-faced boys in elementary school grades to grownup college men sporting beards and mustaches fashionable at the time. Before arriving on campus, students were instructed to bring with them "one neat black suit for Sundays, two other plain suits, three pairs of boots, with sufficient linen [undergarments], stockings, etc." Bright colors and novel fashions in clothing were strictly forbidden. In addition, older students were warned they would not be able to oil their hair, wax their mustaches or splash on sweet scents. Beards and mustaches were permitted for those who could grow them, provided they were nicely trimmed.[17]

FATHER PETER J. GREY TO THE RESCUE

Despite his success in launching the new school, Father Harrington was apparently not a good businessman. Unfortunately, tuition had been set too low to cover expenses, and then it was not always collected. Bills went unpaid, as did the salaries of lay professors. Drastic fiscal reforms were called for if the college would be saved from bankruptcy. Alemany therefore decided to replace Father Harrington with Father Peter J. Grey, only six months after Saint Mary's opened its doors. Grey was well known in the archdiocese for his business acumen. As a result of shrewd land sales, the lean, cigar-chomping priest had been able to accumulate a personal fortune of $100,000.[18]

At the time Father Harrington was replaced, Father Richard Brennan succeeded Father Gallagher as second in command. Although Father Grey was the actual head of the institution, he was instructed by Alemany to pass on to Brennan the major responsibilities normally handled by a college president of the day. "I think he [the vice-president]," Alemany wrote to Father Grey, "should be devoted chiefly to the advancement of pupils in the classics, regularity, and discipline, catechetical instruction, confessions of children and the like." However, Grey was to handle all financial matters. It seems clear that the archbishop's chief purpose in changing presidents was to improve the school's bottom line as quickly as possible. Nonetheless, Alemany urged the new president to move gently and justly. "The success of the college in the future will depend much on the success of the coming months," the archbishop told him, "and I am sure you will devote all your energies to the same, acting always with mildness and fairness, dealing kindly towards all."[19] This may have been asking too much of a man fairly described as "stern, severe and dictatorial."[20]

Father Grey took office at Saint Mary's two days after Christmas in 1863 while remaining pastor of Saint Patrick's Church downtown. The new president insisted that delinquent parents pay up back tuition and board and then raised existing charges and added new ones. Grey had the archbishop send this curt note to a mother who had not paid her son's fees: "Your little boy, Willie, was left with us sometime since. I hope you will pay his board and tuition fees, which amount to $100.00 last June."[21] In addition to collecting delinquent payments, Father Grey wisely increased the tuition and board by $25 a year. Moreover, he decreed that it would have to be paid six months in advance or else parents would be hit with a 10 percent surcharge. A new prospectus forthrightly announced: "On account of the low pension, St.

Father Peter J. Grey, the second president of Saint Mary's College. *Courtesy of Christian Brothers Archives, Napa.*

Mary's College is run on a rigid cash principle, and failure to pay will cause the removal of a boy."[22]

In attempting to keep down expenses, Grey neglected to reimburse several lay professors for work done during vacation periods and sometimes held up their regular salaries for lack of funds. When he threatened to reduce the wages of Professor John Spottiswood, the aggrieved academician asked Father Croke, who had originally negotiated his contract, to intervene on his behalf. Croke replied that he would observe past salary agreements but that future "circumstances may demand a different arrangement and I hold myself free to vote for whatever I may deem most conducive to the interests of the institution and at the same time fair towards all who labor for its progress and success." Having tramped the Gold Country for two years collecting funds to build the college, Croke firmly held onto the hope of its eventual success, notwithstanding the school's current perilous financial situation. "From what I heard of the last examination," he told Spottiswood, "I think we have reason to be proud of St. Mary's as a literary establishment. Its advantages to the public are not yet duly appreciated but time will effect a change. Then I hope St. Mary's can afford to be generous towards those who labor with zeal and profit in the noble cause of education. Meanwhile, we must be satisfied with a moderate supply of U.S. coin and plenty of prayers."[23] Unhappy with the vicar general's equivocal response, Spottiswood decided to seek redress from the archbishop himself but got nowhere.

In a desperate effort to raise revenue, Father Grey made the serious mistake of accepting as charges of the college delinquent boys who had been remanded to it by the Police Courts of San Francisco. Civic leaders had evidently concluded that Saint Mary's would provide a more humane environment for the young offenders than the iron cages of the House of Correction, which was located just across from the college campus in a gulch through which Islais Creek wended its way to China Basin. In addition, the City of San Francisco would have to compensate Saint Mary's for their upkeep and care, contributing as a result to its empty coffers. A cellblock was built on campus to house the delinquents. Neither the professors nor the regular students welcomed the presence of these additional "students." The faculty finally went on strike, and a "free-for-all fight" broke about between the paying students and the court referrals "in which some unpleasant things happened."[24] One can only imagine what they might have been. For good reasons, Father Grey was forced to close down the "semi-reformatory department."

Dismal Prospects

By 1868, inefficient management, financial woes, declining enrollment and faculty turmoil threatened to sink Saint Mary's College. In his laudable effort to provide a college education for young men of modest means, Archbishop Alemany made the serious, although understandable, mistake of setting the college's fees at a level too low to cover daily operating expenses, much less to help lighten its heavy mortgage. Relying on volume rather than proper pricing, he had "anticipated that [a] large attendance will make the institution self-sustaining, even at this low rate [of $150 per annum],"[25] but he was sadly mistaken. After the novelty of a low-fee college wore off, the enrollment at Saint Mary's began to plunge, along with its revenues. Just five years after it opened, Alemany's college had reached the point of no return; only a religious order of teachers, trained to operate an institution of higher learning, could hope to bring some order out of the chaos and set the institution, at long last, on a solid academic and financial foundation.

Chapter 2

Renewed Hope

· ·

*The Arrival of the De La Salle
Christian Brothers, 1868–1879*

B efore Saint Mary's College opened in the summer of 1863, Archbishop
Alemany had tried for many years to obtain the De La Salle Christian
Brothers to staff it. Back in the winter of 1856, he had written to Brother
Facile Rabut, the visitor (or provincial) of Canada and the United States,
requesting that a foundation of the order be made in faraway California.
Brother Facile said he was willing to send a few brothers out West, provided
the superior general, Brother Philippe Bransiet, also approved. Consequently,
on May 4, 1857, the archbishop sent an urgent letter to the motherhouse in
Paris seeking "to have a colony of your good Brothers [in San Francisco]
for the good education of our young men."[26] The superior general's reply,
explaining that he did not have enough experienced, English-speaking
brothers at his disposal, did not reach Alemany. The archbishop sent a follow-
up letter early in 1858, pleading once again that a small band of brothers
be sent to his remote frontier archdiocese. "I would…request of you," the
archbishop stated, "to be so good as to let me know, whether we may expect
within a year or so, to see our boys gathered together and protected from
danger and temptation under the good guidance of the Brothers of the
Christian Schools."[27] This time, the superior general's response reached the
archbishop, but again it was negative. "Unfortunately, I still find myself,"
Brother Philippe wrote back, "in the same penury of subjects as at the time
of my first letter."[28]

For the next eleven years, Alemany tried by every conceivable means
to secure a few Christian Brothers. He sought the aid of the president of

All Hallows Seminary in Ireland, the archbishop of Dublin and the new vicar apostolic of Marysville, but to no avail. To anyone who would listen, Alemany predicted that the Christian Brothers would enjoy a bright future "on these promising shores of the Pacific."[29] Increasingly desperate, the archbishop even recruited a couple of young Irishmen and sent them to the Christian Brothers' novitiate in New York for training, but they apparently never returned. Despairing of obtaining De La Salle Christian Brothers, Archbishop Alemany begged the Xaverian Brothers in Belgium to take over Saint Mary's, but that scheme also came to naught.

Refusing to admit defeat, Alemany decided in the spring of 1867 to enlist the assistance of Pope Pius IX during a visit to Rome. The pontiff listened to the archbishop's plea that a few Christian Brothers be dispatched to San Francisco and ostensibly instructed Cardinal Alessandro Barnabo, prefect of the Congregation of the Propagation of the Faith, to write a letter to Brother Philippe in support of the request. It reads:

> *On the part of his Grace, Archbishop Alemany of San Francisco, very pressing prayers have been addressed to this Sacred Congregation for the purpose of aiding him to provide for the instruction of the numerous children of his Archdiocese who are unable to obtain a Catholic education. Unless this lack is supplied by a sufficient number of qualified teachers, it can easily be seen that grave dangers will menace the Catholic cause in that country. Therefore, considering the matter conscientiously as is my duty, I write to you to request you strongly to come to the aid of the excellent Bishop, as much as in your power, by sending to his Diocese as many suitable Brothers of your congregation as may satisfy his pressing needs.[30]*

Armed with this official letter, Alemany visited the superior general in France to personally present his case. The archbishop handed Brother Philippe the letter from Cardinal Barnabo and told him that it had been written "by the direction of the Holy Father." The archbishop further stated that his only purpose in sailing to Europe was to obtain Christian Brothers and that he had been promised a few of them several years earlier. Undeterred, the superior general tried to explain that the recent Civil War had depleted the institute's houses in the United States, leaving few brothers available for new foundations. But Alemany's response was unflinching: "It must be done. It must be done." Worn down, Brother Philippe finally gave in. A little later, he entrusted to Brother Facile, now his assistant superior general for North America, all of the "details" for mounting the mission to California.[31]

Father Croke, acting as Alemany's vicar general, traveled to New York City to open negotiations with Brother Patrick Murphy, the visitor of the New York District (Province) who had been assigned the task of assembling the pioneer group by Brother Facile. A meeting was held on April 13, 1868, to work out the practical details for the new foundation; in addition to Father Croke, Father William Quinn, vicar general of the New York Archdiocese, represented the interests of the Archdiocese of San Francisco in these talks. All concerned agreed that Alemany would pay $800 for the passage of the brothers to California and give them the keys to Saint Mary's once they arrived. The major unresolved question was whether the brothers would be required subsequently to pay a rent each year, as Alemany would have preferred. The New York provincial held back on this matter because he did not believe that an anticipated increase in the annual tuition and room and board from $175 to $200 would enable his confreres to pay a yearly rent and, in addition, raise sufficient revenue to establish a province of the order in the Far West. Without a clear-cut agreement or contract, the brothers prepared to sail for California. Some of the pioneers later would conclude they had been sent on a fool's errand.

BROTHER JUSTIN AND THE PIONEER BAND

From schools in Maryland, New York and New Jersey, Brother Patrick chose nine brothers for the mission to San Francisco: the leader was Brother Justin McMahon. A vigorous man of thirty-four, he had migrated to the United States from his native Ireland as a teenager, fleeing famine and fear of civil war. The other pioneers, all bearing the names of obscure, long-forgotten saints bestowed on them at the time of their investiture, were Brothers Cianan Griffin, Sabinian Downey, Dimidrian Higgins, Gustavus Fitzpatrick, Emilian Petermann, Pirmian Moller, Genebern Steiner and Adrian Denys Gaynor.

Gifted with a magnetic personality, Brother Justin would soon become one of early San Francisco's most prominent civic leaders and a spokesman for the large Irish community. That he was perfectly suited by temperament and talents for the role of a founder there can be no doubt. However, higher superiors in the East may have had another reason for sending him on his challenging new assignment. As director of important communities in New York and Maryland, Brother Justin had acquired the reputation of a rabble-

Brother Justin McMahon, the first brother president of Saint Mary's. *Courtesy of the Christian Brothers Archives, Napa.*

rouser. He was even charged with being the ringleader of a clique that had opposed the appointment of Brother Patrick as the visitor of New York. At this distance, it is not clear why so many confreres were unhappy with Brother Patrick, but higher superiors went forward with his appointment anyway. In the spring of 1868, Brother Facile sent a letter to Brother Patrick with this interesting suggestion: "I think you must take advantage of certain vacancies to destroy this spirit of rebellion. You will have a perfect occasion to do so in making [the new foundation in] California."[32] In other words, the San Francisco venture would provide an ideal opportunity for him to remove one of his chief critics from the scene. Apparently, this is exactly what happened, and New York's loss became California's gain.

The first leg of the journey to San Francisco began on July 16, 1868, when the nine pioneer brothers boarded the *Ocean Queen* in New York City bound for the Isthmus of Panama. Just before departing, the nine pioneers were treated to a delightful surprise. A flotilla of boats, one carrying the acclaimed Manhattan College band, began to approach the large passenger ship shortly before it was scheduled to sail. Excited passengers, including the brothers themselves, rushed to the rails to see what all the commotion was about. Soon enough, they glimpsed the figure of the college's prefect, Brother Jasper Brennan, attired in his flowing black robe and crisp white *rabat*, shouting from the deck of the college yacht and waving a broad and fond farewell to his departing confreres. When the school band struck up "Home, Sweet Home," some of the brothers on deck began to cry. "The cheers and waving of hats and handkerchiefs on board the College boats," a contemporary account tells us in the flowery prose of the day, "fully attested the cordial love the escorting party entertained for the departing Brothers, and this enthusiasm of their friends affected them so deeply that not a few had to withdraw from the public gaze to give vent to their feelings in secret."[33]

When the *Ocean Queen* docked at Aspinwall (Colon), the nine brothers disembarked and crossed Panama by train and wagon. Reaching the Pacific Ocean, they boarded the *Montana*, a Pacific Mail side-wheel steamer, for the last leg of their journey to San Francisco. After almost a month of travel on the sea and by land, the small missionary band arrived at their destination on August 10. On the following Sunday, Archbishop Alemany told the congregation of Saint Mary's Cathedral: "I made a journey of twenty thousand miles to get the Brothers. I have at last succeeded. Let us give thanks to God!"[34]

The Brother Who Would Be Mayor of New York City

Upon landing in California, Brother Adrian Denys (William J. Gaynor was his secular name) decided to leave the institute and return home to New York City. By one means or the other, he never told anyone how, Gaynor made his way back to the East Coast. There he read for the law, passed the bar and became a justice of the New York Supreme Court. In 1909, Gaynor won election as mayor of New York City on the Tammany Hall ticket. Despite its endorsement, Gaynor was a dedicated and incorruptible reformer. Once in office, he pushed for mass transit, eliminated tolls over the East River Bridge and rooted out corruption in city government. In 1910, Mayor Gaynor was shot by a city employee who had been dismissed from office. He survived, but the bullet remained lodged in his neck for the next three years. Gaynor's would-be assassin was sentenced to twelve years in prison for also shooting one of the mayor's companions and later died in an insane asylum. Immediately after the shooting, a surging tide of public sympathy led supporters to speculate that Gaynor might one day be elected governor of New York and maybe even president of the United States. But the mayor spurned higher office. His health impaired by his wound, Gaynor died of a heart attack in 1913 at sea. He left behind a wife and seven children.[35] The bloody photograph of the assassination attempt has since become a classic example of on-the-spot pictorial journalism.

The Brothers Take Charge of the College

Led by their indefatigable provincial and president, the pioneer brothers immediately set out to revitalize Alemany's diocesan college. Appointments were quickly made; duties were specified. Brother Justin became president and senior class professor and Brother Cianan, vice-president and head of the junior class. Named prefect of studies and discipline, Brother Genebern was put in charge of the sophomore class. As the unofficial head of the Religion Department, Brother Sabinian wrote an explanation of the famous Baltimore Catechism. He also taught the freshman class and served as the school's bookkeeper and treasurer. Brother Emilian was appointed to teach Latin and Greek, becoming the first in a long line of classics professors. In the early years of the college, there was little academic specialization, and a brother would be assigned to teach nearly all subjects to an entire class. Brother Gustavus was appointed to head the separate and distinct Commercial Department. Brother Pirmian, who had once studied for the priesthood, taught modern languages and supervised the chapel; in a short time, he would become the first novice master of the new district. Young Brother Dimidrian was quite ill when he arrived, so he was given such light jobs as a prefect, gardener and domestic worker. He died of tuberculosis on February 7, 1869, just eight months after coming to San Francisco.

Not long after arriving at the outlying campus, Brother Justin initiated a program of physical improvements that required a few years to complete. Over the cloister on the second story of the main building, he had a "wide veranda" or gallery enclosed in glass to afford protection during recreation periods from the damp fogs that crept over the college on almost a daily basis. Brother Justin tore out the basement under the

Brother Cianan Griffin, one of the pioneer brothers and later president. *Courtesy of the Christian Brothers Archives, Napa.*

28

The main Saint Mary's College building and the wing that was built. *Courtesy of the Christian Brothers Archives, Napa.*

adjoining refectory building and used the granite and brick to line walkways around the college, which were much needed on rainy days. According to Brother Cyril Ashe, "at the southern end of the main building were erected handball ball courts which were ever occupied, [and] at the eastern end of the north wing was built the Brothers' Community over the new kitchen. West of the addition, and at a right angle with the building, he [Brother Justin] built a row of shacks in which were housed the Chemistry room, laundry and smoking room." All of these new structures were of the "temporary type" because the Brothers assumed that one day the school would be completed or that its "severe climate" would compel them to move to a better location.[36] A year or two after arriving in San Francisco, Brother Justin purchased a large bell for Saint Mary's from the Meneely Bell Company of Troy, New York. It was carried to San Francisco in 1872 by a freighter around Cape Horn and then mounted in the lantern tower of the wing building in 1872.[37]

Under the direction of the Christian Brothers, Saint Mary's College got off, literally speaking, to a shaky start. On October 21, 1868, a severe earthquake, between 6.8 and 7.0 on the Richter scale, shook San Francisco in the early morning, killing three persons and badly damaging the customhouse downtown. The tremor terrorized the students at Saint Mary's College, as chimneys tumbled and loosened bricks fell to the ground. The young men, who were eating their breakfast when the quake struck, fled from the school buildings, and classes were suspended for a day.[38] Reporting on the effects of the earthquake, the *San Francisco Morning Call* said of the city's frightened inhabitants: "Men, women, and children rushed onto the streets—some in a state of semi-nudity—and all in the wildest state of excitement. Many acted as if the Day of Judgment had come. For a time the excitement was intense, and the panic was general."[39] In addition to the "Great San Francisco Earthquake," as it was then called, the pioneer brothers had to cope with a smallpox epidemic that carried away hundreds of San Franciscans, not to mention the myriad problems presented by a school facing serious financial problems and a depleted student body. By the time the Christian Brothers arrived at Saint Mary's, enrollment had dwindled to just thirty-four students and the faculty to only two professors. Some of the missionaries became quite discouraged by these challenging conditions and wanted to abandon the mission and return to the more civilized East Coast. Brother Justin, who "did not share their sentiments," did his best to lift their spirits. He even told them he would stay in San Francisco and carry on the work alone, if necessary. This exhortation had its desired effect, and the pioneers "soon took heart again."[40]

By Christmas 1868, enrollment at Saint Mary's had increased to 80 students and by the next term, to 160. A year later, it stood at 225. Of this number, between 30 and 40 were commuters from San Francisco proper or neighboring towns such as San Mateo. Alemany's diocesan college would soon become the largest institution of higher learning in the state, outstripping even the University of California in Berkeley, which was founded in the same year the Christian Brothers arrived in San Francisco. In a report to the superior general in 1876, Brother Justin noted that Saint Mary's College "is fully equal to any two colleges in the state, including that of the Jesuit Fathers, who have the finest buildings, best climate and accommodations in the State."[41]

Academic Developments

On May 28, 1872, Brother Justin obtained Articles of Incorporation for Saint Mary's College from the State of California. On the following day, the school was able to award its first two bachelor's degrees: James J. Lawler received a bachelor's of science, and Jackson Alpheus Graves, a bachelor's of arts. Although now a full-fledged "university," Saint Mary's continued to offer academic programs for both grammar and high school students. In 1875, 80 youngsters were enrolled in what was called the "preparatory department." Some 160 older boys were taking more advanced courses, which were divided into three departments: the commercial, scientific and classical. The first enrolled 90 students; the second, 40; and the third, 30.

It is important to emphasize that early day Saint Mary's was not a freestanding college as it is today. In fact, the purely collegiate division, excluding the commercial department, was the smallest of its four component parts. Much the same thing could have been said of both Saint Ignatius and Santa Clara, as well as of most institutions of higher learning in the United States in the second half of the nineteenth century. In the absence of a large number of high schools, colleges and universities in most parts of the country incorporated prep schools to ensure a steady stream of students.

During the early years, Saint Mary's students were subjected to public examinations at the end of each semester. Open to visitors, they took place over a ten-day period just before the Christmas break. According to the *San Francisco Guardian* of December 29, 1877, the commercial, business and accounting students acquitted themselves "remarkably well." However, the "special class" in dogmatic and moral theology faced a tougher task. They were examined by the archbishop and by members of the clergy entirely in the Latin language, which they were expected to speak fluently. After the examinations, Alemany congratulated the brothers for the "happy results" and prayed that Saint Mary's "might long continue in the glorious work of dispensing the blessings of a liberal and Christian education to young men of the Pacific Coast."[42] In later years, brothers wisely decided to drop these public examinations. They were rather pretentious affairs, intended more to impress parents than to educate students.

Commencement ceremonies at the end of the school year were quite different from their contemporary counterparts, during which much time is spent reading off the names of graduating seniors and awarding various prizes and honors. In the late nineteenth century, "the English college on the American frontier told about itself at the annual commencement exercises. There and then the curriculum went on display: Students exhibited, professors paraded, parents applauded."[43] During Brother Justin's years as president, graduation ceremonies were held at Platts Hall, Union Hall and the Grand Opera House in downtown San Francisco. They featured numerous musical selections by the college orchestra and choir; instrumental and vocal solos;

poetry readings, orations and elocutionary recitations of various kinds; and, on occasion, even a short dramatic presentation. High church and civic leaders, including the archbishop and governor of the state, regularly attended these long and lavish affairs. Frequent attendees would favorably or unfavorably compare one commencement to another, prompting Brother Justin to continually search for novel features and entertainments but "of a style commensurate with the noble motto of the institution."[44]

FACULTY CREDENTIALS AND PROMINENT PROFESSORS

Of the twenty brothers stationed at Saint Mary's in 1875, only one had earned a bachelor's degree. He was Brother Benezet Thomas Kane, a young Irish immigrant who entered the province's first novitiate in the fall of 1870. Before joining the institute, young Kane had earned a degree in civil engineering in his native Ireland. After a year of religious training, Brother Benezet Thomas immediately became vice-president in charge of curriculum and spiritual exercises. In August 1871, Brother Justin told Brother Patrick back in New York that "young Kane is a splendid scholar and as pious and as simple as he is talented. He teaches logic, civil engineering, and French."[45] Unlike Brother Benezet Thomas, the other brothers didn't enjoy the benefit of a four-year college education. During the nineteenth century, there were no collegiate houses of study in any of the districts of the institute in the United States. Most candidates spent only a year or two in a novitiate training program before teaching, many as teenagers. As a result, almost all of the Christian Brothers at Saint Mary's in San Francisco were self-educated.

One of the most accomplished faculty members in the 1870s was Father William Gleeson, MA, professor of Latin and college chaplain. Having once ministered in India and Turkey, Gleeson was fluent in Hindustani, Persian and Arabic. While residing at the Mission Road campus, in 1872 he published a two-volume *History of the Catholic Church in California*. Hubert Howe Bancroft, an early historian and ethnographer of California and the Pacific Coast, praised Gleeson for his scholarship, although reservedly: "Gleeson is not so able a writer, and fell into more errors [than fellow California historian Franklin Tuthill]," Bancroft noted in the first volume of his *History of California*, "yet as a Catholic priest he has some superior faculties. He read more of the old authorities, went more fully into details, and was quite conscientious; and he has given us a pleasing and tolerably accurate picture of mission life and annals."[46]

The most famous and influential faculty member at Saint Mary's in the early years was the political economist and social reformer Henry George. A largely self-educated man but an original thinker of the first order, he taught courses and conducted public examinations at Saint Mary's College during the 1870s and became a close friend of the president, Brother Justin.[47] Born in Philadelphia in 1839, George came to California as a young man of nineteen; later, he worked as a reporter and editor for newspapers in Sacramento, San Francisco and Oakland. As a keen-eyed journalist, he began to think seriously about the glaring economic inequalities of American society. It seemed strange that during an age of great material progress there should be so much poverty. In *Progress and Poverty: An Inquiry into the Cause of Industrial Depressions and of Increase of Want with Increase of Wealth: A Remedy*, written while teaching at Saint Mary's[48] and published in 1879, George attempted to confront this conundrum. He concluded that land monopolists were taking unfair advantage of the rising value of property. They merely sat on their land waiting for its price to rise, while small farmers could not afford to work their fields any longer. George's solution was to impose a confiscatory tax on the unearned increment resulting from the natural rise in the value of property. This "single tax," he believed, would supply the government with all the funds it needed and reduce the tax burdens on labor and production. High taxes on land would also force owners to put it to productive use or to sell it to those who would, thereby increasing employment for workers and spreading wealth more evenly.[49] One of George's followers invented a parlor game called the Landlord's Game in 1904 to illustrate his theories; later, with some modifications, it became the perennially popular board game called Monopoly. Various sources claim that Brother Justin assisted George in writing his famous treatise.[50]

The growing income gap in the United States and recent proposals to revamp the federal tax code have revived interest in George and in his theories and proposals. In the 1880s, George campaigned not only for greater economic equality and tax reform but also for free trade and electoral reform. "The last succeeded," writes Harvard historian Jill Lepore. "That is why, on Election Day, your polling place supplies you with a ballot you mark in secret. This is known as the Australian ballot, and George brought it back from his voyage half way around the world." When the great reformer died in 1897, 100,000 mourners filed past his bier in Grand Central Station. The *New York Times* declared at the time, "Not even Lincoln had a more glorious death."[51]

If George's single tax had also been enacted, Father Peter J. Grey, the second president of Saint Mary's College, would never have been able to accumulate his personal fortune. Alemany himself hoped to capitalize on lucrative land deals to lighten his heavy debt load. In his history of Saint Mary's, Brother Cyril Ashe comments, "Mortgages, loans, and real estate deals kept him in continual anxiety."[52] Perhaps with his vow of poverty, working-class origins and direct experience of injustice in Ireland, Brother Justin was much more open to George's ideas, if he did not actually help to formulate them.

Student Life

By contemporary standards, student life at Saint Mary's College in the early years was highly regimented. The school day began at six o'clock in the morning with rising and morning prayer and ended with lights out at the early hour of eight thirty in the evening. Interspersed during the day were time slots for meals, classes, recitations, study halls, recesses and recreation periods. This semi-monastic regimen continued well into the twentieth century. Saint Mary's students had little opportunity to board a Front Street, Mission and Ocean Railway horse-drawn car or a much faster San Jose–San Francisco steam railroad coach for the short trip to the diversions of downtown. According to an 1868 college prospectus, "No leave of absence will be granted to Students during the course of the Scholastic Year, except for the usual Christmas holidays. Neither will any Students be allowed to leave the College Grounds, unless accompanied by one of the Professors, or by his parent or guardian."[53] Day students from the city proper enjoyed relatively easy access to the college because the Bernal Station of the steam railroad was located nearby, and the fare from San Francisco proper was only twenty cents.

The college offered its students an outstanding program in music, under the direction, from 1868 to 1904, of the bewhiskered Professor Frederick Schorcht. Formerly of the Prussian Imperial Palace Band, he later served as a bandsman during the Civil War, despite his detestation of war and violence. At Saint Mary's College, he conducted both the orchestra and choir. It was said that Schorcht would begin orchestral pieces by stamping twice and then intoning, "Vun, two and start fiddlin'!"[54] One of the most popular clubs on campus in the early days was the Justinian Debating

The Saint Mary's Orchestra, directed by Professor Schorcht. *Courtesy of Saint Mary's College Archives, Moraga.*

Society. Its president was lay professor Lawrence Taafe, who also taught mathematics. One of his grateful students later described Taafe as "whole-souled" and "fair-minded,"[55] which are quite nice things to say about a former teacher.

The Christian Brothers introduced an intercollegiate sports program to Saint Mary's College shortly after their arrival. In 1872, the year the institution received its charter, it fielded its first varsity athletic team, a nine-man baseball squad, which adopted the mythical phoenix as its emblem and team name. Four members of the team traveled with the San Francisco Centennials to Philadelphia in 1876 to participate in a tournament held in conjunction with the city's Commemorative Exposition celebrating the 100th anniversary of the signing of the Declaration of Independence. The California team beat some of the best amateur and semiprofessional teams in the East, proving the worth of West Coast baseball and the quality of the college's players. In the late nineteenth century, the game of baseball, invented before the Civil War and avidly played by the troops, was the most popular sport on college campuses; only later would football and basketball steal the limelight. Mark Twain remarked that baseball was "the very symbol, the outward and visible expression of the drive and push and rush and struggle of the raging, tearing, booming nineteenth century."[56]

Brother Justin, the Ideal Nineteenth-Century President

Brother Justin presided over Saint Mary's as if he were the headmaster of an English public school. Manly and forthright, he was strict with his charges but fair, too. One of his first acts as president was to abolish the "Black Hole of Calcutta," a place of punishment for "exceptionally unruly boys" located in the school's basement. Henceforth, it served as a trunk room.[57] Rather than strike students, Brother Justin preferred to discipline them by making them feel ashamed of themselves for misbehaving. It was the president's custom to assemble the boys each morning for a daily exhortation. By all accounts, Brother Justin was a brilliant orator who would have made a fine lawyer. Earnestly, he would urge his students at these morning assemblies to live according to the maxims of "honesty, integrity, the clean life, earnest endeavor, respect for parents, and due regard for the rights of others."[58] In all respects, Brother Justin was the exemplar of the nineteenth-century college president known for his paternalism, wisdom and benevolence. These were the days before a great deal of academic specialization, large administrative bureaucracies or numerous departments; as a result, a college president could function as the dominant presence on campus, in direct, personal contact with all the students. This certainly was the case with Brother Justin.

In a college prospectus published in 1868, shortly after the brothers arrived in San Francisco, Brother Justin stressed the importance of creating a community of learners at Saint Mary's, an important characteristic that has defined the school ever since. "Living in the same house, sitting at the same table, presiding at the recreations, and, as far as possible, forming a family circle with their pupils, it is reasonable to suppose," one reads, "that the Brother can easily gain their confidence, and thus be in a position to direct them more successfully in their studies."[59]

Brother Justin believed that students had certain rights that ought to be respected. On one occasion, first graduate Jackson Alpheus Graves was given a severe penance by his Latin instructor, Father Gleeson, for asking him unwittingly for the meaning of a vulgar word "not fit for polite ears." Graves had been duped by fellow student Gwin Maynard, a mischievous lad and also the grandson of Senator William M. Gwin of the vigilante days, who shot at a political foe in a duel, missed and killed a donkey instead. After providing Graves with all four parts of the offending verb, Gleeson turned to him and said, "Oh, Graves, I did not think that of you! Before you go home, translate, parse, and scan the first twenty lines of that Ode of Horace beginning with the words, '*Qui fit Maecenas ut nemo quam sibi sortem,*' etc." The crestfallen student went out to the porch outside the classrooms, found a desk, pulled out his grammar and lexicon and buckled down to the task. Brother Justin came upon him laboring in the late afternoon, slapped him on the back (he was that kind of guy!) and asked, "Well, well, what are you doing here?" Assured that Gwin Maynard would not be punished, Graves explained what had happened. The president was more than sympathetic. "You are innocent of any wrong," he told the student, after listening to his story. "That's a frightful task. You will be here all night." Then, in a flash, he added, "Wait a minute. I will send you to Brother Amelian [*sic*; Emilian, another Latin teacher] to help you out." Informed of the student's predicament by Brother Justin, the good-natured classical scholar, only twenty-six years old at the time, came up to Graves laughing and poked him in the ribs. Brother Emilian then proceeded to translate the passage as fast as Graves could write it down. Shortly, the young lad slipped it under the door of Father Gleeson's room, as earlier directed. Brother Justin later spoke to the priest, who admitted that he had acted hastily and even apologized to Graves, who feeling guilty confessed in turn that he had gotten help from Brother Emilian. The old Latin teacher and young Graves remained steadfast friends. Later in life, translating the Ode of Horace stood Graves "in good stead." An "eminent priest" claimed that Saint Mary's boys "did not know anything," betting a young lady twenty dollars that not one of them could translate the very piece of classical literature that Graves had earlier struggled with. She told Graves, he translated the ode and she became twenty dollars the richer.[60]

Chapter 3

At the Crossroads

·······························

The Latin Question and Possible Eviction,
1868–1879

D uring Brother Justin's tenure, Saint Mary's faced two serious crises: one was curricular and the other was financial. The first involved the question of whether the Christian Brothers would be able to maintain the college's classical department or be forced to close it down because of the institute's arcane rule banning the teaching of Latin. The second involved the heavy mortgage the school was carrying and Archbishop Alemany's consequent efforts to sell the college to the brothers or force them to pay an annual rent. There was even an outside chance they would be evicted from the Mission Road campus if the dispute over the school's and the archdiocese's debts was not settled to the archbishop's satisfaction.

TEACHING THE CLASSICS

The academic structure and program of studies at Saint Mary's in the 1870s mirrored nineteenth-century trends in American higher education. As mentioned earlier, the collegiate curriculum was divided into three distinct departments: the commercial, classical and scientific. According to a report Brother Justin compiled in 1876, the commercial curriculum aimed to "give a thoroughly practical education, one that will fit the student for business." Among the courses offered by this department were everyday mathematics, banking, bookkeeping, commercial correspondence and business buying and selling. In contrast to the mostly vocational courses offered by the commercial division, the classical course embraced Greek, Latin, mathematics, composition, rhetoric, logic, metaphysics, moral philosophy, history and general literature. Occupying pride of place, the classical course could be traced back to liberal arts colleges at Oxford and Cambridge, to colonial colleges in New England and to the *Ratio Studiorum* of the Jesuits. The Latin and Greek program was based not only on the methodical acquisition of these ancient languages but also on the honing of mental skills through the traditional liberal arts. The goal, repeated frequently, was to educate and form both intellectually and morally the "whole man." Students enrolled in the science curriculum pursued a course of studies similar to that of classical students, except that they took language courses in Spanish and French and also took more courses in higher mathematics.[61] Without the necessity of mastering difficult ancient tongues, far more students pursued the BS than the BA.

Venturing into the field of classical education placed the Christian Brothers at Saint Mary's in technical violation of their Rule and Constitutions because the teaching of Latin and Greek had been strictly forbidden to them by their founder, Saint John Baptist De La Salle.[62] His reasons for imposing a strict ban on Latin and Greek in the late seventeenth century were both practical and precautionary. In the first place, he did not want his followers to study the classics for fear that they would abandon their humble calling as schoolmasters and become priests. La Salle's second reason was directly related to the purpose of the institute he was seeking to establish. He wanted to provide the poor boys of France with a basic religious and secular education, and he did not believe that either the teachers or students of his charity schools required knowledge of Latin and Greek to meet this pressing need. It made much more sense to teach street urchins elementary subjects and religion in their native tongue.

Although La Salle's reasons for banning classical studies were entirely reasonable, his precautions against their acquisition or propagation seem quite the opposite, at least from our present perspective. In the *Memoire sur L'Habit*, he even raised the question of whether or not candidates who had studied Latin should be admitted to his brotherhood. Fortunately, he favored their acceptance, but "only on condition that they never again pursue advanced studies" upon donning the religious habit. Most of his early disciples had precious little formal education, so this was not a major disqualification. The following line was deleted from the original manuscript of the treatise on the religious habit by a different hand in different ink in later years: "Those who make up this Community are all laymen without a classical education and possessing but average intelligence."[63]

When the founder and the early brothers wrote the Rule of the Institute, they made certain that the regulations against studying and teaching Latin and Greek were spelled out in minute detail. Among other things, Chapter XXVI of the Rule of 1718 stipulated that brothers who had already learned classical languages would be required to act as if they had not; that no brother would be permitted to teach Latin inside or outside of one of the institute's schools; that no brother would be permitted to read a book in Latin or to speak Latin unless absolutely necessary; that no Latin books, except for the Divine Office, would be kept in any houses of the institute; and that no brother less than thirty years of age would be permitted to read a book with Latin on one side and the vernacular on the other, if a dangerous penchant to learn this ancient language had been detected in him by his religious superiors.[64]

Down the decades, the European brothers faithfully followed this strict ban on classical languages not simply because of their respect for the Rule and Constitutions but, more important, because of the congruence of this prohibition with the class structure and educational needs of the Old World. It was obviously not necessary for Christian Brothers to master difficult ancient languages if they taught reading and writing to poor boys in charity schools. But neither was it necessary for them to teach classical languages if they taught in the institute's middle-class boarding schools that proliferated in France throughout the eighteenth and nineteenth centuries. In such schools, the older sons of the bourgeoisie preferred to study practical subjects such as banking, agriculture, commerce, engineering and seamanship. Middle-class parents were quite pleased with the modern approach to education that came to be identified with the De La Salle Christian Brothers. They did not believe that the liberal arts education provided by the Jesuits was well suited to the special needs of their more practical-minded offspring, who looked forward to pursuing careers in the world of business, commerce, engineering and the military.[65]

Responding to quite different social and ecclesiastical conditions in the United States, the American Christian Brothers expanded the institute's traditional educational mission to include classical studies. American bishops wanted to use the brothers' schools to prepare candidates for the priesthood in a missionary land heavily dependent on foreign-born clergy. Since priests were in such short supply, bishops preferred to keep them close to the people in parish work. As Brother Justin later explained to higher superiors in Europe, Alemany "wanted the Priests for his missions; hence the change of teachers for the college" from diocesan clergy to the Christian Brothers.[66] Obviously to prepare students for sacerdotal studies, Latin needed to be taught. The bishops also urged the brothers to offer classical languages in order to help immigrant Catholic boys enter the liberal professions of law, medicine and teaching in an upwardly mobile society. This also required the teaching of Latin and Greek because at the time American higher education was decidedly classical both in philosophy and content. Mastery of classical languages was the indispensable requirement for earning a bachelor of arts degree.

When Brother Justin and the other pioneers arrived in San Francisco in August 1868, the local Catholic newspaper perceptively declared:

> *Indeed, the original object of the venerable founder of the Brotherhood of Christian Schools was to provide for the primary education of the poor in human knowledge and religion, and to this end, the efforts of his followers are still mainly directed. The wants of American society, however, needing such a modification of the rule, in this country, as would permit of the addition of higher studies to their system of education, the Brothers have established colleges throughout the country, in which the full course in humanities [or the classics] is taught. In St. Louis, in New York, in New Orleans and at Pass Christian, in Mississippi, and Rockhill, Maryland, the full course of instruction given in other Catholic colleges is taught in their seminaries, and such will also be the case in Saint Mary's College.[67]*

This statement did not refer to gratuitous grammar schools or fee-charging technical boarding schools but to true liberal arts colleges. Such institutions were entirely new to the institute.

The close relationship between teaching classical languages and the preparation of candidates for the priesthood can be glimpsed in the alumni lists of Saint Mary's College from 1863 to 1900. During this period, 270 students were graduated from the college, and 26 of them, or nearly 10 percent, later received holy orders. The brothers at Saint Mary's were pleased that their college had not only produced many priests but also broadly educated young men who entered the professions and public life and thereby contributed to California society. As previously noted, the first student to graduate from Saint Mary's with a BA in 1872 was Jackson Alpheus Graves; he later became one of California's most prominent bankers. A year later, Bartley Oliver and Henry V. Reardon received BA degrees, and Charles M. Weber, son of the founder of the city of Stockton; J.T. Murphy; and William Shipsey received BS degrees. Weber became a California assemblyman, Murphy a bank commissioner, Reardon a district attorney of Butte County, Shipsey an attorney and Oliver a teacher at Saint Mary's and later a benefactor.

When Brother Justin arrived at Saint Mary's, the school's classical curriculum presented him with a kind of crisis of conscience. He had had explicit permission, despite institute regulations, to teach Latin at Assumption Academy in Utica, New York, but he was uncertain whether he needed to obtain a fresh authorization to continue this instruction in San Francisco. He decided to consult his confessor, who happened to be a local Dominican. The priest told Brother Justin:

> *The fact that your Superior General has sent you to take charge of a college presumes permission to study Latin. The Church would not permit you to be the head of a college where Latin is taught, if you did not know it...Meanwhile, it is your duty to call your superior's attention to the situation, and it will be necessary for him either to withdraw you from the College (something he cannot do since you have been sent there by the order of the Holy Father) or to give you blanket permission to teach Latin, and not only to you, but [to] as many of the Brothers who are needed to conduct the college effectively.*[68]

Doubtless, Brother Justin sought and received permission from higher superiors to teach Latin.

The Crisis of 1879

When the brothers arrived in San Francisco in 1868, both the archdiocese and its college were drowning in debts. Utterly desperate, in 1872 Alemany attempted to sell Saint Mary's to the federal government for the purpose of a naval hospital on the West Coast. The scheme fell through because the fog and wind of Bernal Heights were not good for convalescing sailors. It appears that the archbishop planned to use some of the projected selling price of $150,000 to build a college for the brothers in Oakland across the bay. Failing to strike a deal with Washington, Alemany began negotiating with Brother Justin and the superior general in Paris for a possible sale of

Saint Mary's to the institute. These negotiations reached a critical point in the spring of 1879. "Pressed very hard by the Director of Hibernia Bank to pay back interests compounded," Alemany told Brother Justin on March 12 that he was "obliged to demand" that he purchase Saint Mary's College with eight or ten acres around it at $75,000 (or the entire tract for $100,000 more) or else pay him $25,000 with interest from "the time you commenced to use it." As if to soften the blow, the archbishop added: "With the good disposition and great energy which God has given you, and the encouragement which I would most willingly give, I believe you can realize any of the above proposals." And then with startling candor, he concluded: "I need not repeat that I would most cheerfully abstain from the above demands, but I have no alternative if I wish to save the diocese from disgrace and disaster."[69]

Although Brother Justin did not believe that Archbishop Alemany would finally force the brothers out of Saint Mary's, he nonetheless began drawing up contingency plans in the spring of 1879 in the event that he did. He purchased a new site for a novitiate in Martinez so that Saint Joseph's Academy in Oakland would be able to accommodate the younger boys then enrolled at the Old Mission Road campus. He also made plans to reassign displaced brothers to other educational institutions in the area, including various parish schools in San Francisco and Saint Agnes Academy in Stockton.

Just as the Christian Brothers were resigning themselves to the possibility of leaving Saint Mary's College, Alemany radically reduced his demands, now asking only for an annual rent. In April, the archbishop wrote to the superior general: "I find that I must ask in justice some monthly or yearly amount from your Brothers on account of St. Mary's College." Although Brother Justin was "all that could be desired," he naturally preferred to use the school's profits for the benefit of the district, the archbishop continued, "and I would fully and heartily concur with him if I were not too embarrassed [financially]. I therefore have to apply to you for some…equitable consideration on the subject."[70] The superior general was amenable.

The problem then became settling on an amount acceptable to both parties. Higher superiors asked Brother Justin to submit a financial report on the college indicating the amount of salaries being paid, infirmary costs, tuition revenue and income from seasonal crops. He provided this accounting in June, along with this comment: "You require these details with a view of seeing how much rent we can pay without injury to the proper management of the college. I must say in all candor and sincerity, we cannot pay any." However, in view of the archbishop's dire financial straits, the president agreed that some effort should be made to assist him. Perhaps $1,000 in rent and an additional $1,000 for taxes and insurance would be a reasonable amount, but certainly no more.[71]

The motherhouse agreed to the president's proposal. At first, the archbishop accepted the figure of $2,000, but later he changed his mind. In June 1879, he wrote directly to the superior general, bypassing Brother Justin: "I have reflected and consulted on this affair and it appears that considering the great sums that I was forced to borrow in order to complete the building of St. Mary's College and the enormous interest paid over many years, that I should receive $2,500 each year."[72] Further negotiations for a suitable sum therefore became necessary. Brother Justin was upset that he had been left out of the loop. He also believed that the archbishop had sufficient means, if he were a little more patient, to resolve his financial problems. Nonetheless, the president was willing to raise the total package from $2,000 to $2,500 a year—with about $1,000 of this amount to be paid directly to the government in taxes.[73] Alemany declined to accept this new offer, preferring to pay these taxes himself from the funds given to him by the brothers, although he did reduce the total amount required of the college by $200. The archbishop even made a thinly veiled threat in the spring of 1880 to evict the Christian Brothers from Saint Mary's if they did not comply with his latest demand. "I am anxious," the archbishop told the superior general, "to establish a seminary for educating priests; but I do not know yet when, and where. In case that I would need St. Mary's College for that or any similar institution, I would not take any step without first having an understanding with you…"[74] In the face of being expelled from the Old Mission Road campus, the California Brothers decided to meet all of the archbishop's demands, namely and finally, to pay him $1,500 in rent plus taxes and insurance. However, a financial statement in the Christian Brothers archives in Rome indicates that from 1881 to 1884, the archbishop billed the college for only $1,000 in rent each year. Evidently, his tight financial bind had loosened during this period.

Given the college's debts and Alemany's demands, in 1879 Brother Patrick Murphy (now the American assistant superior general for the United States) urged the brothers in California to seriously consider leaving Saint Mary's College voluntarily. It might be better to concentrate on that "special field" where the brothers had more experience and better training; that is, on ordinary parochial grammar schools. Brother Patrick pointed out to the California visitor that the Jesuits were already conducting a college in San Francisco and were building a new campus on Van Ness Avenue. This new school would surely pose a serious "challenge" to Saint Mary's College.

Rumors were also circulating that the Oblates were coming to California either to establish a college of their own or a seminary. (Various men's orders in the Catholic Church are called Oblates; the reference here is most likely to the Oblates of Mary Immaculate, a congregation to which Father Peter J. Grey once belonged.) With a tinge of bitterness, Brother Patrick told Brother Justin that even though the Christian Brothers had "opened the field" in California, others were coming to "gather [in] the harvest." The American assistant's chief concern was that "the clergy always support corporate bodies such as the Jesuits and Oblates" in preference to the Christian Brothers, who were not ordained priests. Under these developing circumstances, the brothers could quietly retire from the field of university-level education, knowing that other religious congregations could readily take their place. "It is preferable," Brother Patrick declared, "to withdraw now when you are able to do it honorably, leaving the whole area your debtor, than to see the college perish later as the result of a poor administration or of contrary influence [from other religious orders.]" If it were necessary to withdraw from the college, personnel could be sent to those parishes in San Francisco that were willing to offer them a residence, but under no circumstances should the province open any more boarding schools or colleges.[75] They were just too much trouble. Inasmuch as Alemany's financial position improved, the brothers in California were able to remain in the field of higher education. It is important to note, nonetheless, that they came close to being forced out of it or leaving it on their own.

Brother Justin Leaves Saint Mary's College

In the fall of 1879, Brother Justin received an order to return to the East Coast, where he was to be installed in the more prestigious post of visitor of the New York District and de facto president of Manhattan College. Two years earlier, Alemany had succeeded in reversing a similar summons by convincing the superior general that the college and the district would not do well under anyone else. As he bade farewell to his confreres, the first brother president of Saint Mary's College and first visitor of the San Francisco District could depart with the satisfaction of knowing that he had succeeded in setting both the college and the district on firm foundations. Of course, he did not save Saint Mary's and establish three academies in Oakland, downtown San Francisco and Sacramento and a novitiate in the East Bay all by himself. He had been ably assisted by the pioneer brothers who trekked to San Francisco with him, by those who came later from the East and by those few who had joined the order in California. Nevertheless, the lion's share of the credit for rescuing the college and building the province belongs to Brother Justin.

How does one account for his remarkable success? Perhaps the secret is to be found in his personality. By all accounts, Brother Justin was a lively and enthusiastic man. In his autobiography, Jackson Alpheus Graves notes, "In all my life I never saw a man with as much energy as Brother Justin. He would have made a name for himself at any calling he adopted, had he not been in a religious order."[76]

Both as president of the college and visitor of the district, Brother Justin maintained cordial relations with the local press, which in turn gave Saint Mary's and the Christian Brothers remarkably favorable coverage. Although a consummate promoter, he never employed "boisterous" methods. Not long after the brothers assumed the operation of Saint Mary's College, he arranged for a public academic exhibition at the Old Mission Road campus in order to publicize the school. According to Brother Cyril Ashe, "The members of the Press [were]…conveyed to the College in a barouche provided by Brother Justin and were given every facility for learning the aims of the Institution and were given honor[ed] places in the auditorium. Their reports of the affair were splendid encomiums of the hospitality and accomplishments that were Saint Mary's."[77]

Brother Justin was also adept at establishing and maintaining cordial relations with the local clergy, without being overly subservient. As Brother Matthew puts it, "For him, respect for the cloth did not mean servility to the cloth, nor did he believe that ecclesiastical office endowed the holder with universal infallibility."[78] It was impossible for any priest, including Archbishop Alemany himself, to look this magnetic man in the eye and judge him inferior simply because he was only a lay religious. On the contrary, Alemany came to regard Brother Justin as his right-hand man.

Today, we might describe a man like Brother Justin as charismatic. However, one might not deduce this from old photographs, which picture a round-faced man with an almost bulbous nose, unruly hair and wire-rimmed eyeglasses. Only the firm set of his jaw and perhaps his piercing blue eyes offered hints of his inner drive and determination. The first president of Saint Mary's College may also have been its greatest.

Chapter 4
"The Athens of the Pacific"
·····························
Saint Mary's College Moves to Oakland, 1879–1900

Brother Justin's successor as visitor of the San Francisco District and de facto president of Saint Mary's College was none other than his blood brother, Brother Bettelin McMahon, former president of Rock Hill College in Ellicott City, Maryland. Although sons of the same parents, the McMahon brothers were as different as two men could be. Justin was short and stocky; Bettelin was tall and lanky. "Justin was fiery, mercurial, and active. Brother Bettelin was slow, phlegmatic, and reflective."[79] Lacking either the intellectual power or dynamic personality of his predecessor, he had a hard time filling his brother's shoes. Anyone would have.

Brother Bettelin's most important decision as president was to move Saint Mary's from San Francisco to Oakland. The college catalogue would later boast that "this city, not inappropriately styled the Athens of the Pacific, possesses many advantages favorable to educational accomplishments: the climate is mild and healthful, the surrounding scenery delightful; the city is sufficiently remote from the metropolis, yet easy of access."[80] Although most of the brothers were happy to be rid of the wind and fog of the Old Mission Road campus, a few lamented having to leave a cosmopolitan city like San Francisco for the dirt fields and scrub oaks of the East Bay. As one later remarked, "There is a spontaneity among the people of San Francisco that you do not find anywhere else in the West."[81] It is interesting to speculate that Saint Mary's might have developed into an urban commuter university had it remained in San Francisco, as the city grew up around the once remote campus and provided more shelter against the elements. Brother

Brother Bettelin McMahon, the second brother president. *Courtesy of the Christian Brothers Archives, Napa.*

Joseph Fenlon, who became visitor in the 1920s, pointedly asked in later years, "Why did they move at all? They would, with new buildings, have been better off where they were [on the Old Mission Road campus]—better off in the long run—better off today."[82]

The visitor decided to employ a land agent, one Francis S. Wensinger, in finding a site for the new campus on account of anti-Catholic prejudice rampant at the time in the East Bay. Brother Bettelin finally agreed to acquire an eight-acre plot at Broadway and Thirtieth Streets at the foot of what is now called "pill hill." After much huffing and puffing, the Christian Brothers were able to purchase thirty-two lots for only $22,000. Subsequently, Brother Joseph criticized the selection of such a confined campus: "What a place to build with so much fine land available in those days [in the East Bay]. They had a chance to get a fine, a really large place, right on Lake Merritt for less than they paid for the piece on Broadway."[83]

The cost of the new college building in Oakland was expected to reach $350,000, a princely sum for a province with limited financial resources. At the provincial's direction, the various religious communities of the district, which at the time was made up mostly of poor parochial schools, pinched pennies and came up with a heroic and yet pitiful contribution of $15,000. Individual brothers made gifts from their modest patrimonies and also turned over properties they held in trust, one of which, raffled off at $5 a chance, brought in almost $8,000 for the building fund. Archbishop Patrick W. Riordan, who had succeeded Alemany, and supportive priests did their part to assist the Christian Brothers, as did a number of lay friends, who made donations to the campaign ranging from $180 to $250. One of the latter was the remarkable African American woman Mary Ellen "Mammy" Pleasant, a former slave who is rightly regarded as the "mother of the civil rights movement in California." She used her considerable fortune, inherited from her first husband, to support the abolitionist movement before the Civil War and helped to set up the underground railroad in the Far West. Falling on bad times in later years, Mary Ellen was forced to declare bankruptcy in 1899 and died penniless five years later. A generous philanthropist in her heyday, she was well known for donating large amounts of money to various churches and charitable projects.[84] One of her numerous donations was to the new Saint Mary's College in Oakland. The total collected from her and other donors was less than $100,000, leaving the school once again deeply in debt.

On October 22, 1887, Archbishop Riordan laid the cornerstone for the new school after its foundation had been poured. Before ten thousand spectators, he interned the following inscription, once again anchoring the school in time and place: "This cornerstone was laid by the Most Reverend P.W. Riordan, Archbishop of San Francisco, on the 22nd day of October, in the year of Our Lord 1887, Pope Leo XIII gloriously reigning, Grover Cleveland, President of the United States; R.W. Waterman, Governor of the State, W.R. Davis, Mayor of the City of Oakland."[85] Conspicuous by his absence at the impressive ceremony was Archbishop Alemany, who had returned to his native Spain two years earlier. The founder of Saint Mary's College died in Valencia in 1888 as a simple Dominican friar. Two years after Riordan laid the cornerstone, he returned to Oakland to dedicate the completed campus during impressive ceremonies before a large throng.

THE OLD BRICKPILE

After fulsome speeches, spectators were invited to tour the five-story building designed, it was touted, in the Renaissance architectural style. In Chicago during the 1890s, the noted American architect Louis Sullivan had developed a brilliant new architectural style based on the principle that the "form and layout of a building should follow its function." Unfortunately, this sane concept was not embodied in the plans for the new college building, which were drawn up by a young San Francisco architect, J.J. Clarke. If we can judge by the final product, he knew absolutely nothing about collegiate architecture. Brother Joseph described the "block of a thing" as "one of the poorest planned buildings in the whole state of California."[86] He was not exaggerating. The hulking Oakland edifice looked more like a grand hotel

The Old Brickpile in Oakland, built in 1889. *Courtesy of the Christian Brothers Archives, Napa.*

or a garment factory than a college. Built in the shape of the letter E, with north and south wings, the structure was constructed of 2,500,000 red bricks made by the famous Remillard Company. Not surprisingly, the school was quickly dubbed the "Old Brickpile."

Only a smattering of students from the old campus transferred to the new one in Oakland, so that when Saint Mary's opened in the fall of 1889, it was virtually a brand-new school. Although its curriculum remained as it had been in San Francisco, the survival of richer historical documents from the period provides a more detailed picture of the school's premier classics department. Students enrolled in this program pursued a course of studies remarkably similar to the Great Books Program of the modern Saint Mary's—but with one major exception. They read Homer's *Iliad*, Virgil's *Aeneid*, Sophocles's *Oedipus Tyrannus*, Herodotus's *Histories* and Thucydides's *Peloponnesian Wars* in the original Greek and Latin in which they were written. There is even some indication that the college favored a discussion-based methodology. Insisting that Saint Mary's College offered its "students every facility for acquiring the highest grade of Liberal Education," the college's catalogue declared that "care is taken that every branch [of knowledge] prescribed be thoroughly studied and that nothing be learned by rote." Students discussed topics independent of "the language" of textbooks, criticized one another's "work" and freely offered opinions "on all points open to debate."[87]

The Saint Mary's rugby side in 1909. *Courtesy of the Saint Mary's College Archives, Moraga.*

During the 1890s, Saint Mary's initiated long-standing football rivalries with two neighboring institutions of higher learning. The first was with Santa Clara College. On Thanksgiving Day 1896, the two schools met on the gridiron for the first time in San Francisco's Central Park; 1,500 spectators paid fifteen cents a piece to watch Saint Mary's get plastered, 46–4. Embarrassed by the defeat, Saint Mary's temporarily disbanded its team but returned to the gridiron two years later. The "Saints," as the college's athletic teams were then called, suffered an even worse loss in a second game with Santa Clara, which ended in a free-for-all brawl between rooters on both sides. In November 1898, the college football squad boarded a horse-drawn trolley for a four-mile ride to the much larger campus of the University of California in nearby Berkeley. Once again, it suffered a devastating defeat, 51–0. However, the game marked the inauguration of one of the longest football rivalries on the Pacific Coast. On account of poor performances and serious injuries, Saint Mary's College dropped football at the end of the 1898 season. For several years, the English college sport of rugby took up the slack.

A Catastrophic Fire

In June 1894, Brother Erminold O'Donnell was appointed the seventh president of the college. On his way home from an outing to the brothers' novitiate in Martinez, in the late afternoon of Sunday, September 23, 1894, he noticed from his train window billowing flames and smoke in the distance, but he had no idea that Saint Mary's was on fire until he arrived on scene. The conflagration had started in the waste chute in the center of the building between floors when a worker carelessly emptied hot ashes into it. The brothers were unable to contain the blaze with fire hoses mounted in the building because of low water pressure. As brisk winds began to fan the flames, they were forced to retreat and then give up the battle entirely. As students and bystanders began hauling out everything that was not nailed down, a double general fire alarm was sounded throughout the city. Handicapped by hoses that were too short to reach the building and also by low water pressure, the Oakland Fire Department was unable to bring the blaze under control. To make matters worse, several firefighters arrived at the blaze drunk and therefore incapacitated. Some scientific equipment, a few pianos and museum items were saved from the flames, but three libraries and most of the classroom furnishings were destroyed, and many professors lost their precious lecture notes and books. Fortunately, no students were killed or hurt in the fire. However, seven firemen were burned or cut, none fatally. One was given his last rites after being struck in the head by a burning beam, but he fortunately recovered. The brothers and the boarding students were forced to sleep on the college lawn that night, in sight of the smoldering ruins with the acrid stench of smoke polluting the air. A later assessment of the damage revealed that the upper three floors had been destroyed; the second floor badly damaged, requiring that it be torn down; and the main floor also badly damaged.[88]

Brother Bettelin, the visitor, was in New York City at the time of the fire, preparing to embark for France. He immediately returned to Oakland to assess the damage. Unfortunately, the college carried only $20,500 in fire insurance, when it should have been covered for between $80,000 and $100,000. Given the school's heavy mortgage, district officials had been too eager to save money. They also thought the building was fireproof. To his credit, Brother Bettelin shook off his characteristic lethargy and, according to a confrere, was "moving heaven and earth to rebuild, and have it [Saint Mary's College] ready by the beginning of next year."[89] Fortunately for the Christian Brothers, Archbishop Riordan of San Francisco rushed to their

The Old Brickpile after the fire of 1894. *Courtesy of the Christian Brothers Archives, Napa.*

assistance following the fire. He offered to let them return to the old campus in San Francisco, took up a relief collection in San Francisco and Oakland parishes that raised $15,000 and organized a group of Bay Area businessmen to launch a fundraising campaign to rebuild the school.

The year spent back at the Old Mission Road Campus was not a happy one. The main building was now a parish church, and other parts of the school were being used as a dairy and stables. After a month spent refurbishing the old campus, a relocated Saint Mary's College was ready to reopen, but only barely. On the first day of school, students were forced to carry their own bedsteads and mattresses upstairs or else sleep on the floor. In the process of transferring the school to San Francisco and then back to Oakland, enrollment dipped from 166 to 95, including the loss of between 40 and 50 boarders. One of the pioneer brothers claimed that the fire had set the district back ten years, which is probably an exaggeration.[90]

Headquarters of a Papist Army?

When members of the Oakland Fire Department inspected the college after the fire, they found stacks of muskets stored in the school's basement. These obsolete weapons, purchased from the federal arsenal in Benicia, belonged to the college's "League of the Cross" Cadet Corps. In the 1890s, Saint Mary's sponsored a military training program that attempted to cultivate "manly bearing, habits of attention, and prompt obedience."[91] Clad in Civil War–style uniforms, students would march around the grounds to the barked commands of an army officer named Colonel D. Geary. It was all harmless enough—just a lot of parading under the flag and to the beat of a John Philip Sousa march. However, during the 1890s, the United States was suffering from a periodic outbreak of anti-Catholicism. The American Protective Association (APA), a nativist organization founded in Clinton, Iowa, in 1887, was warning the citizenry of papist plots to overturn the government and kill patriotic Protestants who dared stand in the way. It was rumored that the Old Brickpile was really the East Bay headquarters of a secret Catholic army in training for a coming insurrection. As proof, local Oakland Protestant ministers declared in the pages of the *Occident*, a local APA mouthpiece, that seven hundred rifles had been found at Saint Mary's. This was a gross exaggeration; there were only one hundred in storage. Nonetheless, two Southern California newspapers repeated the spurious

APA claims in March 1895. Brother Walter O'Melia, the president at the time, dashed off a letter to both journals, in which he explained that the cadet program was well known to the public and that its drills were open to anyone who cared to watch them. In short, there was nothing secretive or sinister about the training regimen. "There were and still are some old muskets at St. Mary's College, Oakland," Brother Walter conceded. "Not however,

Brother Erminold O'Donnell, president during the fire of 1894. *Courtesy of the Christian Brothers Archives, Napa.*

such as the soldier would like to have on active duty, nor yet such as the sportsman would wish, for they might prove as disastrous to himself as to the game," he humorously added.[92]

The Latin Question Heats Up, 1858–1900

The success of the De La Salle Christian Brothers in teaching the classics at Saint Mary's and at the other colleges in the United States became a grave concern to the Society of Jesus, which feared that its vested interests in the field of classical education were being threatened. With Darwinian exaggeration, the *Chicago Sunday Times Herald* explained to readers on January 22, 1899, that "since the Christian Brothers opened schools for the classics, the Jesuits have had a fierce struggle for existence, notwithstanding their worldwide reputation and their preeminence in the domain of letters."[93] As a matter of fact, institute schools in this country never posed such a serious threat to the well-established and widely respected educational institutions of the Society of Jesus, but they did offer the Jesuits unexpectedly stiff competition in Philadelphia, Buffalo, New York, Saint Louis and San Francisco as classical educators.

In seeking to suppress the teaching of the classics in the institute's schools, the Jesuits received strong support in the 1890s from the institute's French superiors, who had grown increasingly hostile to the higher-level educational work their American confreres had engaged in now for more than forty years. From 1854 to 1894, the superiors general of the Christian Brothers in Paris had countenanced the teaching of classical languages in the United States. Brother Philippe had sent brothers to take over Saint Mary's College in 1868, and his successor Brother Irlide had granted Brother Justin permission to purchase the school ten years later, even though both men knew that Latin and Greek courses formed an important component of the school's tripartite curriculum. Unfortunately, the willingness of these two leaders to permit educational adaptation in this country was not inherited by their successors. Over time, institute superiors came to regard teaching the classics as a radical departure from the traditional work of the institute to teach the lower classes basic subjects and the middle classes practical courses. They also claimed that it inflated the American brothers with intellectual pride and created, as a consequence, an invidious class distinction between the "patricians" who taught in classical academies and colleges and the "plebeians" who labored in ordinary parochial schools.

After 1894, European superiors demanded that their American confreres concentrate their educational efforts on staffing parochial grammar schools, polytechnic institutes and orphanages. However, the brothers in the United States were being pulled along a quite different educational salient. By 1900, they were conducting no fewer than twenty classical academies and nine university-colleges in which either Latin or Greek, or both languages, were taught as part of a distinctively liberal arts curriculum. As American brothers, including those stationed in California, entered more and more into secondary and collegiate education, their self-image began to change; a significant number came to regard themselves as learned professors rather than simple schoolmasters. Bishop Thomas Sebastian Byrne of Nashville caught this change in self-perception when he told the apostolic delegate to the United States in 1898 that Christian Brothers in this country "though good and obedient religious, are naturally indignant and feel the conditions on which they entered the Society will be essentially changed [if classical studies were banned], since from high grade educators they will pass, owing to the educational requirements of this country, into the category of ordinary humdrum schoolteachers."[94] In common with the students they taught, the brothers also began to rise in the educational world. This novel and unexpected development became a cause of considerable concern to the brothers in the Old World. In 1898, the superior general sternly warned American Christian Brothers in a circular letter that "it would be rash for us …to wish to occupy learned chairs."[95]

Determined to abort the historical evolution of the American brothers toward liberal arts education, the General Chapter of 1894, which was dominated by French delegates, voted to reaffirm the traditional ban against Latin and Greek and compel the Christian Brothers in the United States to close forthwith the classical departments of all of their secondary schools and university-colleges. Appalled by the deleterious effects such a ban would have on the Catholic school system in this country, prominent members of the American hierarchy, led by Archbishop Riordan of San Francisco, petitioned Rome in 1895 to permit the American brothers to continue teaching Latin and Greek, but curial officials turned a deaf ear to their urgent pleas. In 1895, the *Propaganda Fide* supported the French position and ordered the suppression of the classics in the brothers' high schools and colleges throughout the United States. However, the American brothers stalled while awaiting further appeals.

The first came in 1898, when the American hierarchy petitioned Rome to reverse the edict issued three years earlier. Bishop Byrne was deputized to present its united appeal to the highest ecclesiastical authorities at the Holy See. During an exchange of petitions, the head of the institute told curial cardinals that only a few Christian Brothers in the United States were in favor of studying and teaching Latin and Greek. In response, Bishop Byrne promised to deliver the names of at least eight hundred American brothers who wanted to maintain their classical academies and colleges. With the cooperation of brothers throughout the United States, he was able to hold what amounted to a plebiscite on the Latin Question in the spring of 1899. In most communities of the San Francisco District, the brothers were asked to sign petitions that in substance read: "We earnestly desire that our superiors permit the continuance of our Colleges in the United States." Teaching the classics was so entwined with the purpose and future of collegiate education that Latin and Greek were not even specifically mentioned, although the communities at Saint Peter's in San Francisco and Saint James in Vancouver, Washington, were requested to support an even more explicit statement—namely, "we are in favor of the teaching of Latin in our Colleges." The results of the vote show that the overwhelming majority of the brothers of the province voted in favor of the classics. At Saint Mary's College in Oakland, twenty-two brothers, virtually the entire community, signed the petition.[96]

Bishop Byrne's efforts in Rome finally proved futile. Institute higher superiors enjoyed wide influence within the Roman curia and were more adept at ecclesiastical politics than was the inexperienced American prelate, even though he spoke fluent Italian. After six months of fruitless lobbying, Bishop Byrne returned to the United States without a favorable decision in the Latin Question case.

During the winter of 1898 and spring of 1899, members of the institute in the United Sates continued to circulate petitions and issue manifestos demanding the right to continue teaching the classics. These acts of formal disobedience infuriated the superior general of the institute. In July 1899, he decided to draft a severe letter to the Christian Brothers in the United States threatening them with dire penalties if they persisted in advocating the teaching of classical languages. In order to compel adherence to the directives of the General Chapter and the *Propaganda Fide*, the superior general took the added step of requiring all of the brothers in the United States, including those in California, Oregon and Washington, to sign a loyalty oath not to study or teach Latin and Greek or face the prospect of immediate dismissal from the congregation. The oath reads in full: "I, the undersigned, member of the Institute of the Brothers of the Christian Schools, declare that I submit entirely and without reserve to the prescriptions of Chapter

XXVIII of our holy Rules, to Decree IX of the Sacred Congregation of the Propaganda, dated June 25th, 1895, and confirmed by our Holy Father on July 4th following. Wherefore, I promise to follow in all things the directions that will be given by the Most Honorable Brother Superior General relative to the question of Latin in our establishments."[97] If, after seven days, a brother was unable to sign on the dotted line, he was dismissed from the institute; that is to say, he was dispensed from his vows of obedience and poverty but not from chastity.

Fearing that the American brothers would form an independent branch of the institute in the United States, the superior general in France decided, beginning in 1898, to remove from office and send into exile fourteen prominent provincials, college presidents and prominent professors, even to remote locales such as Egypt, Malacca and Ceylon. A few of this number, including Brother Justin, were first summoned to a special commission in Europe and charged with and then convicted of prevarication and disloyalty. Only one of those removed from office refused to be shipped overseas. Brother Felix O'Connor, president of Christian Brothers College in Saint Louis, applied for a dispensation from his vows and was ordained to the priesthood after brief study at the archdiocesan major seminary. In California, Brother Bettelin was removed from office in 1900 and made the director of an orphanage in Troy, New York. Brother Justin would spend the next few years teaching English at a boarding school in Toulouse, France.

Disturbed by these developments, the American hierarchy decided in 1899 to send Archbishop Riordan of San Francisco to Rome to present yet another petition in favor of the classics. Responding to pressure from the superior general, his assistants and the procurator-general of the institute, as well as from the Society of Jesus, the Congregation of the Propagation of the Faith rejected Archbishop Riordan's latest memorial and confirmed the ban on teaching Latin and Greek late in 1899. Pope Leo XIII ratified this decision early in the following year. The case was now finished. In communicating Rome's ruling, the superior general told his American confreres that "it is the desire of the Sacred Congregation that the Technical and Commercial Schools of the Brothers be developed in the United States of America," but not classical or liberal arts colleges.[98]

Chapter 5

A Technical College

·····························

Saint Mary's College Changes Its Colors, 1900–1923

From 1900 to 1923, Saint Mary's College faced one difficult challenge after another. Among other setbacks, it suffered serious damage from the San Francisco Earthquake of 1906 and another destructive fire in 1918. In that same year, the United States Army commandeered the campus and turned it into an armed camp to train officers for the First World War. Worst of all, Latin and Greek classes could not be taught after 1900, forcing the college to shut down its most prestigious academic department for the next twenty-three years. As a result, Saint Mary's became more like the technical institute European superiors wanted it to be.

After the elimination of Latin and Greek, Christian Brother colleges in the United States were forced to make major adjustments. However, all of the brothers' advanced institutions were able to retain their charters because of curricular changes taking place in American higher education. A letter sent to the alumni of Manhattan College declared reassuringly, "In dropping Greek and Latin we are partially following in the footsteps of leading colleges of the land, such as Columbia, Harvard, and Cornell where the study of the dead languages is elective and not required as a condition for admission to the schools of medicine and law…"[99]

At Saint Mary's, the brothers decided to teach Latin surreptitiously. In December 1903, the newly founded school newspaper, christened the *Collegian*, carried the following boxed advertisement: "Thomas F. Phelan, A.B. Teacher of Latin and Greek. 2042 Broadway, opp[osite] St. M[ary's] C[ollege]. Terms Reasonable." Phelan was a lay professor and coach of the school's baseball team; his wife made the shapeless black robes the brothers wore in class. The couple lived on the upper floor of a two-story building at the address given in the advertisement. In a small shop on the first floor, Brother Albian Benedict Dooley, not Thomas Phelan, secretly taught the classics to Saint Mary's students from across the street. When the Jesuits got wind of this clever but harmless arrangement, they reported the brothers to Archbishop Riordan, who was forced, against his own deepest wishes, to close down the little storefront Latin school. Brother Albian Benedict was crushed by this outcome. "They [the Jesuits] pulled the rug out from under me," he told a former student, "and I have never been the same since."[100] It is not known which Jesuit protested. However, on May 19, 1906, an Italian Jesuit teaching at Saint Ignatius College, Father Gregory Leggio, wrote the following entry in his diary: "It appears that the Christian Brothers have a house across the road from the college in which Latin is taught. They seem to evade the decision of the Holy See, a decision which is surely clear enough."[101]

New Academic Programs

Responding to the ban of Latin and Greek and to emerging trends in American higher education, Saint Mary's established several new educational programs in the period from 1900 to 1923. The most important was the new School of Engineering that was inaugurated in 1902; it offered specialized programs in metallurgy, hydraulics, assaying and mining. When Brother Florinus Peter Doyle became president in 1910, he decided to expand and upgrade the Commercial Division. Ten years later, Brother Gregory Mallon established a new School of Foreign Trade. For the first time, a business program at Saint Mary's offered its graduates college degrees rather than certificates. In 1912, Brother Fabrician Pellerin set up two new departments in art and architecture. During the period when classical studies were banned, Saint Mary's also ventured into the field of pre-professional education, adding a pre-medical program in 1910 and a pre-legal program two years later. In 1922, Saint Mary's established a School of Education to train future teachers; in conjunction, young Christian Brothers were enrolled in a new collegiate scholasticate. Candidates would now ideally receive a college education before being sent out to teach. In all these curricular changes, one sees increasing emphasis on the technical, vocational, pre-professional and scientific aspects of higher education. In important respects, Saint Mary's

A photograph of the banking class at the Old Brickpile. *Courtesy of the Christian Brothers Archives, Napa.*

was beginning to move in the direction of a small comprehensive university, especially after it added an evening law school in the mid-'20s. However, its small campus precluded any dramatic expansion.

BROTHER FABRICIAN AND THE SPORTS FRATERNITY

Of all the presidents in the early twentieth century, the best qualified in terms of previous experience and broad outlook was Brother Fabrician Pellerin. Formerly president of La Salle College in Philadelphia and Saint John's College in Washington, D.C., he was the last Latin Question exile to return to the United States. Charming, urbane and scholarly, Brother Fabrician assembled a distinguished faculty, appointed the school's first full-time librarian and sponsored several distinguished lectures on campus. As a committed academician, Brother Fabrician harbored serious doubts about the value of intercollegiate athletics; this brought him into sharp conflict with the athletic buffs on campus. According to the October 1911 issue of the *Collegian*, he told the assembled students in his first presidential address

Brother Fabrician Pellerin, president of Saint Mary's. *Courtesy of the Christian Brothers Archives, Napa.*

Brother Agnon McCann, athletic buff. *Courtesy of Christian Brothers Archives, Napa.*

that they "did not come to Saint Mary's to run the quarter-mile or play in the backfield on the football team. You came to college to study. St. Mary's exists for the formation of moral and intellectual habits, not for the display of physical powers."[102]

Brother Fabrician's tough talk riled Brother Agnon McCann, the irrepressible advisor of the sports fraternity on campus. An avid sportsman, he leaned to the notion that one of the college's primary purposes was to produce star players for major-league baseball teams, which it did to an extraordinary degree in the early decades of the last century. Among the big league stars who had played for the school were the legendary Harry Hooper, Duffy Lewis, Walter Mails, Bill Simpson and Dutch Leonard.

Ironically, the athletic program at Saint Mary's expanded during the very years Brother Fabrician served as liberal arts dean and then as president. From 1901 to 1913, the college's baseball team won twelve consecutive championships in the old California-Nevada

Members of the Phoenix baseball team in 1904. *Courtesy of the Saint Mary's College Archives, Moraga.*

Baseball League. During the 1907 season, the Phoenix nine compiled the nearly unbelievable record of twenty-six victories, no losses and one tie. By 1910, fourteen former Saint Mary's baseball players had made it to the Major Leagues, a record few other colleges or universities could match. A year later, in 1911, Saint Mary's College upset the Boston Red Sox in a preseason game. Four baseball players who had attended the Old Brickpile were starters, and one was a reserve player, for the Boston Red Sox or the Philadelphia Phillies in the World Series of 1915.

The expansion of intercollegiate athletics at Catholic colleges accelerated early in the last century. "Faced with growing competition for both students and resources from the rapidly expanding land-grant colleges and nonsectarian sectors of the higher-education community and concerned that their visibility was dimming as quickly as their moral authority," sports historian Dr. Paul Zingg argues, "these schools increasingly turned to their intercollegiate programs as agents of institutional identity and promotion. Although football and later basketball would be the sports of choice in this effort for Saint Mary's…baseball put the college on the athletic map first and set the tone for all subsequent forays into the world of intercollegiate athletics."[103]

Alumnus Randall Andrada shows in his history of Saint Mary's football that Brother Fabrician had good reason to be concerned about the negative impact intercollegiate athletics were having on Saint Mary's. In 1911, the year Brother Fabrician became president, the Phoenix baseball team swept a series with archrival Santa Clara. Partly as a result, a dispute broke out between the two schools over the eligibility of certain players; it became so charged that both institutions threatened to sever athletic relations. Efforts by both Saint Mary's and Santa Clara to determine which players should be suspended and when athletes should be required to sign up for classes were not successful. According to Andrada, "Intense negotiations between the presidents of the two schools failed to break the impasse. Rather than submit to arbitration, the schools terminated an athletic relationship already forty years old." The sports public in the Bay Area was quite upset with this unfortunate and unexpected outcome.[104] Tired of fighting those brothers who favored intercollegiate athletics, Brother Fabrician left Saint Mary's after his three-year term expired and took up a new academic post in the Midwest.

CELEBRATIONS AND FESTIVALS

In 1913, Saint Mary's College celebrated its fiftieth anniversary. Brother Fabrician presided over a week of commemorative events, beginning with a gala picnic and dance in nearby Hayward on May 13. A mile-long car caravan, festooned with flags and pennants, wended its way to the grounds. On the following day, students staged a gala circus in the overflowing campus stadium, featuring clowns, acrobats, equestrians and animals. The next big event was Alumni Day, when old grads came back to the Old Brickpile to walk down memory lane. On the fourth day of "Jubilee Week," religious ceremonies took center stage with the celebration of a Pontifical High Mass at Saint Mary's Cathedral in San Francisco. Ensuing days were devoted to graduation ceremonies for the various educational departments.

On the occasion of the tercentenary of Shakespeare's birth, Saint Mary's held a month-long commemoration in April 1916. Almost all English courses were devoted to lectures and readings of his famous tragedies and comedies. As Brother Matthew colorfully puts it, "The great Elizabethan was read and debated inside and outside of class, quoted in the locker room

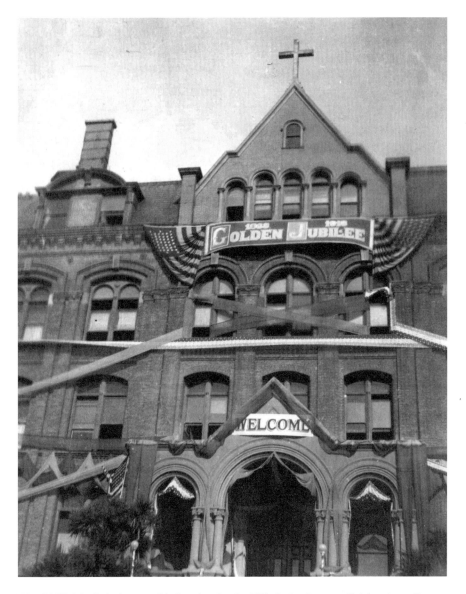

The Old Brickpile is decorated in bunting for the Fiftieth-Anniversary Celebrations. *Courtesy of the Saint Mary's College Archives, Moraga.*

and parodied in the dining room."[105] On May 3, a gala Shakespearean festival was held on campus, featuring orchestral selections, a rendition of the "Songs of Shakespeare" by a noted tenor, orations, recitations and the presentation of a scene from *Richard II*.

Five years after the Shakespeare Month, Saint Mary's honored the six-hundred-year birthday of the Italian poet Dante. For the occasion, English professor Brother Leo Meehan wrote a three-act play entitled *The Wing-Bearer*, which was staged at the Oakland Auditorium Opera House and the Columbia Theater in San Francisco. A local theater critic praised the production for its realism.

Upgrading the Faculty

During the early decades of the last century, Saint Mary's was fortunate to count among its faculty a small number of outstanding Christian Brother teachers. The most distinguished of the lot was English professor Brother Leo Meehan. A short history of the college written in the 1920s declared that "no individual Brother has done so much for the welfare and uplifting of St. Mary's as Brother Leo. His name and worth have spread not only over California but over the entire country."[106] Brother Leo was not only a gifted teacher but also a novelist, playwright and noted lecturer. In 1914, he was able to attend the Catholic University of America for advanced studies. After only a year of study, he was granted an unusual DHL (or doctor of humane letters) degree. One confrere claims that Brother Leo took courses in Hebrew, Scripture and English, another that he spent most of his time writing, reading and lecturing. Both agree that he wrote a dissertation on Shakespeare's historical plays that was later published.[107]

Like most of his confreres, Brother Leo Meehan was largely a self-educated man, notwithstanding his year in the nation's capital. Early in the twentieth century, only a handful of brothers held bachelor's degrees. Brother Fabrician was distressed by this state of affairs. He felt that in the future a college teacher would need to have a master's or even a doctorate. Never reluctant to crack the cake of custom, the president decided to grant four or five of his confreres BAs, based on their many years of independent study, devoted teaching and accumulated odd courses, believing that they had by such nonconventional means "acquired and achieved as much as and more than many a graduated professor in secular colleges and universities."[108] Later, this dubious method of granting degrees became standard practice, especially in adorning presidents with academic credentials they had never really earned.

For his part, Brother Leo McKinnon, one of the recipients, did not think that he deserved an ersatz degree. Confronting the brother charged with lettering the diplomas, he demanded that his own be handed over to him. After three refusals, Brother Leo broke into the rickety cabinet where the degrees were being stored, found his and tore it into little pieces, branding it the "bull in the China shop."[109] In 1920, Brother Leo was given the opportunity to study for a regular master's degree in engineering at Catholic University. He doubtless kept that diploma with pride, although his true love was and always would be poetry and the liberal arts. When the Latin Question inquisitors visited Saint Mary's in the late 1890s, Brother Leo hid the school's classical language books under his bed so they would not be confiscated or destroyed.

Fire, Earthquake and War

During the period when the classics were banned, Saint Mary's College was hit hard by two natural disasters. The first was the San Francisco Earthquake of April 18, 1906. The three hundred residents of the Old Brickpile in Oakland were severely shaken by the temblor, running in panic out of the five-story brick building. On account of its solid foundation and thick walls, the structure did not sustain major interior damage. However, vintage photographs reveal considerable exterior damage, especially to the entrance stairs and porch. Some chimneys also collapsed, along with the south-side gable. Students pitched in to remove the debris, and school was cancelled for a few days. Always short of funds, the college carried no earthquake insurance.

On May 7, 1918, disaster struck again. For the second time, Saint Mary's went up in flames. The fire, caused by a student experimenting with chemicals, could not have come at a worse moment. The draft and the labor demands of war industries were threatening to drastically cut the school's enrollment, and the costs of food and fuel were mounting. As earlier, the Oakland Fire Department was hampered by low water pressure. For a time, firefighters were unable to spray water on the top floors. As a result, they had to drag long hoses up several flights of stairs, attach them to inside water mains and then begin to douse the flames. The brothers organized squads of students to retrieve as much as could be salvaged from the burning building. When the fire was finally brought under control after a five-hour fight, President Brother Gregory Mallon gathered the students in the adjoining field house, which had not been touched, and told them that classes would be cancelled for the last two months of the school year and that graduation exercises

Damage to Saint Mary's following the 1906 San Francisco Earthquake. *Courtesy of Christian Brothers Archives, Napa.*

Ruins of the fire of 1918. *Courtesy of the Christian Brothers Archives, Napa.*

would be conducted at nearby Holy Names College. In an emotion-filled voice, he continued: "Twice we have been knocked down before, but we have come up smiling and we will meet this blow with renewed determination to go on…We shall begin classes on the first of next September."[110] The students greeted his courageous announcement with a wild cheer.

Damage to the building and its contents from the fire and the water used to fight it totaled a quarter of a million dollars. The college carried only $50,000 in insurance; once again, officials had proved penny-wise and pound-foolish. Citizens of the Bay Area responded to the tragedy with great generosity. According to Brother Matthew, "In the evening, the Red Cross under Charles J. O'Connor, director of the Pacific Coast Division, furnished cots for some students in the gymnasium while others found shelter in private homes or in Idora Park, a nearby amusement center."[111] After an exasperating delay, the visitor, Brother Calixtus Curran, finally approved a fundraising campaign to rebuild the college. Archbishop Riordan contributed a check for $10,000. However, it was his auxiliary bishop, the Most Reverend Edward J. Hanna, who galvanized Bay Area business leaders for a campaign to rebuild the college. In the ballroom of the Saint Francis Hotel in San Francisco, he insistently declared, "We cannot allow St. Mary's to become a thing of the past. St. Mary's must not go. Therefore, I make appeal for your help."[112]

The campaign for rebuilding funds was a smashing success. In the East Bay, two hundred door-to-door solicitors sold coupons for ten cents each, stamped with the words "Buy a Brick" for Saint Mary's College. These certificates were similar to the War Savings Stamps then being sold around the country to help defeat the "Horrible Huns." In a widely distributed pamphlet, unnamed Protestants urged citizens not to help rebuild Saint Mary's College but instead to send their "dimes and dollars" to the American Red Cross. This tactic backfired when the local press reminded bigots that hundreds of Saint Mary's students were fighting and dying in the trenches of France. Approximately 856 students fought in the Great War, 200 returned wounded and 15 gave their lives. The college regularly met its war loan drive quotas and assisted "in the patriotic propaganda of the [Creel] Committee on Information."[113] Brother Leo employed his golden voice to sell war bonds.

True to his word, Brother Gregory reopened the Old Brickpile in September 1918. A month later, the federal government turned the Oakland campus into an armed camp. Two hundred students were inducted into the army and placed under the authority of the Student Army Training Corps, or SATC. Other colleges and universities across the country were also taken over by the national government to train officers. By the fall of 1918,

Members of the Student Army Training Corps. *Courtesy of the Saint Mary's College Archives, Moraga.*

140,000 men were enrolled in the United States Army at 525 institutions of higher learning. These new recruits were provided with tuition, board and clothing, as well as a thirty-dollar monthly allowance. For approximately two months, Saint Mary's boys rose to the blare of a bugle and marched to class in close formation. Captain Samuel A. Purviance was named commandant of the Old Brickpile. The brothers themselves were "militarized" and given new titles and responsibilities such as "Instructor in Map Reading and Navigation." The federal government reimbursed the Christian Brothers for the use of the campus and covered the salaries of all faculty members. In the long run, the SATC program encouraged colleges to teach more practical courses and enhanced the social value of higher education. In early 1919, with the end of the war, Saint Mary's was able to return to its regular curriculum, which included arts and letters, civil engineering, commerce and high school courses, but still no Latin or Greek.

The General Chapter of 1923

In 1923, a General Chapter of the institute was scheduled to convene in Belgium, where the motherhouse was then located, the Christian Brothers having been expelled from France. The American delegates drafted another petition to teach Latin and Greek. To old arguments, they added an important new one—namely, that the brothers were being pushed into secondary schools and colleges where Latin was taught, as sisters were replacing them in parochial schools and the government was taking over social welfare institutions.

For his part, the intransigent French superior general was determined that the vexing Latin Question would not even be raised on the chapter floor. The circular announcing preparations for the worldwide conclave stipulated that matters that had been previously discussed and settled would not appear on its agenda. However, this instruction was illicit because the General Chapter was empowered to consider any matter it chose to, even fundamental points of the Rule and Constitutions. Once informed of his mistake, the superior general immediately sent out a correction

The firm determination of the American brothers to air the Latin Question at the General Chapter was clearly evident when Brother Fabrician, the former president of Saint Mary's College and one of the two living "exiles," was elected by the brothers of the New York District as one of their delegates, despite his advanced age of eighty. Doubtless, they elected him out of respect for the memory of his fellow "exiles," who had suffered and died before seeing the day of their vindication. This gesture of solidarity and remembrance was both noble and touching. Brother Justin had often prayed that he would live long enough to see Latin and Greek restored to the curriculum, but his prayer would not be answered. In late February 1912, the brothers at Saint Mary's received word of his death from a stroke.

Shortly before the chapter opened, Pope Pius XI, a classical scholar and paleographer, decided to take matters into his own hands. Through his secretary of state, Cardinal Pietro Gasparri, the pontiff sent a letter to the superior general that virtually ordered the Christian Brothers to teach the classical languages to young men from all social classes, and not only in the United States, but also throughout the world. The pontiff decreed that in the

> *presence of an ever-growing and urgent want felt in different countries, and in consideration of the far-reaching changes which modern times have made in educational programs and statutes, and also in view of the*

larger participation of all classes of society in all kinds of studies…the Institute of the Brothers of the Christian Schools ought, henceforth, extend its teachings to classical studies, as it has already done with success to the higher educational sciences, even in behalf of the well-to-do classes.[114]

Despite affirming the founder's charism and defending past papal decisions—tropes that were to be expected in a document of this kind—the supreme pontiff had, in effect, radically redefined the educational mission of the institute in the modern world. The pope's use of the phrase "well-to-do classes" is frankly jarring, considering the institute's original mission to teach the economically poor. A leading historian of American higher education has rightly concluded that "the directive's importance as the final resolution of the Latin Question obscures its larger significance as a confirmation of what to Saint John would have been a *far more significant departure* from the Institute's foundational charism, the education of the poor."[115] In short, by affirming the historical development of the institute in the United States, the pope's letter changed not only the curriculum of the brothers' schools but their clientele as well. Over the decades, the American brothers had succeeded in turning the order on its head, which is precisely why the French brothers had fought so long and hard to stop the teaching of the classics. They knew perfectly well how high the stakes were.

Courses in Latin immediately returned to the college's catalogue; those in Greek appeared a few years later and were less numerous. However, the lifting of the ban on Latin had a more immediate and long-term effect on the district's high schools than on Saint Mary's College. During the booming '20s, bishops across the country were building numerous Catholic secondary schools, and it was commonly held that Latin was an excellent trainer of young minds, beginning in the freshman year. On the collegiate level, modern languages, business courses, science programs and the liberal arts in English were much more in vogue. The pope's decree came just at the moment when Greek and Latin had largely lost their hold on the curriculum of American colleges and universities. History, as life itself, is filled with ironies.

Chapter 6

A Second Spring

··

Saint Mary's College Moves to Moraga,
1923–1928

Prospects for Saint Mary's College brightened during the Roaring Twenties. The pope's letter lifted the spirits of the brothers on the West Coast; after decades of discouragement, the sense of a beckoning future returned. Later in the '20s, a dynamic new visitor, Brother Joseph Fenlon, decided to relocate Saint Mary's from its cramped campus in downtown Oakland to a verdant canyon in rural Contra Costa County. This gave the school a badly needed new lease on life. The decade itself, when America moved from the farm to the city, was marked by prosperity, progress and peace. "A second spring" was about to bloom for the country, the province and the college.

THE MADIGAN ERA BEGINS

Saint Mary's returned to the gridiron in 1915, after the rules of the game had been changed at the behest of President Theodore Roosevelt, safety equipment had been introduced and the forward pass had been added. Two years later, the football team won eight games, lost one and tied one. Its biggest victory was a 7–0 defeat of the University of Southern California Trojans. However, World War I slashed the size of the student body by two-thirds, and in 1920, the undermanned squad lost to the neighboring University of California by the lopsided score of 127–0. After cancelling the remainder of the schedule,

Edward Patrick "Slip" Madigan, the football coach. *Courtesy of Saint Mary's College Archives, Moraga.*

college officials gave serious thought to eliminating football. Instead, in 1921, Brother Gregory Mallon, the president, decided to hire a new coach. Twenty-five-year-old Edward Patrick "Slip" Madigan, who had had great success at Columbia Prep in Portland, Oregon, was named to lead the Saints football team. In his college years, Madigan had played for the legendary Knute Rockne at Notre Dame. At the time Slip was hired, Brother Gregory told local sportswriters: "The boy coming to college selects his school largely because of its athletic prowess, as reflected in the sporting pages. We pedagogues may like to think otherwise, but we are only deceiving ourselves."[116]

Brother Gregory lured Madigan from a career in law with a handsome offer. According to Brother Josephus Mangan, he "signed 'Slip' for $7,000 per year plus 10 percent net gate…[T]he professors would have fainted had they known the terms."[117] During his early years at the Old Brickpile, Madigan's share of gate receipts did not produce much income; however, by the mid-'20s, these commissions began to mount steadily, until in the next decade he became one of the highest-paid football coaches in the entire nation. Madigan would also become one of the most notorious and newsworthy.

In a few years, he built Saint Mary's into a football powerhouse. In 1926, the Saints scored an impressive 26–7 victory over the University of California before sixty-seven thousand fans in Memorial Stadium in Berkeley. Pat Frayne, a young sportswriter for the *San Francisco Call-Bulletin*, opened his account of this remarkable feat, given the earlier staggering loss, with this memorable line: "The Lone Horseman [running back Boyd 'Cowboy' Smith] and the Galloping Gaels trampled the Golden Bears of California last Saturday in a flurry of speed and strength."[118] The new nickname stuck, and Madigan applied for a copyright within a year.

Brother Gregory Mallon, the president who hired Madigan. *Courtesy of the Christian Brothers Archives, Napa.*

Of all the games Saint Mary's played in the 1920s, the most socially significant was the 1927 tussle with Stanford University. In his saga of Saint Mary's football, alumnus Randall Andrada offers a perceptive account of the contest. He begins by noting that the two schools were mirror opposites. Occupying an arcaded stone campus situated on some eight thousand acres dubbed "the farm," Stanford University enjoyed both a large endowment and a national reputation. In contrast, debt-ridden Saint Mary's College was confined to an eight-acre campus in downtown Oakland and housed in an antiquated building rightfully, if affectionately, called the "Old Brickpile." Stanford was non-sectarian; Saint Mary's was staunchly Roman Catholic. Stanford had been built by the Big Four railroad magnate Leland Stanford, in memory of his deceased son. Saint Mary's had been established by a Spanish missionary archbishop to train future priests and safeguard the faith of Irish Catholic immigrants. The respective coaches of the two schools were as different as the institutions they represented. Madigan was a brash, enterprising Irishman, controversial and colorful. Glenn S. "Pop" Warner of Stanford was an ex–Ivy Leaguer, austere and accomplished.[119]

From the start of the game, Saint Mary's dominated, resulting in a 16–0 victory for the Gaels. Saint Mary's had succeeded in beating the mythical national champion of the previous year. Observers called the contest a religious war. The Protestant Warner, who despised Knute Rockne and the Notre Dame shift, reputedly told his players, "Get those Roman sons-

The program of the brutal Saint Mary's–Stanford football game in 1927. *Courtesy of the Saint Mary's College Archives, Moraga.*

of-bitches." One of the rougher Saint Mary's players, Ike Frankian, was taunted by an opposing Stanford lineman as a "Roman ass," even though he was not Catholic. The game symbolized the decade-long cultural conflict between nativist Americans and immigrant stock, a conflict also reflected in the fight over prohibition, the rise of the Ku Klux Klan and the enactment of immigration restriction legislation. "The Catholic working-class boys who played football for Saint Mary's," Andrada writes, "were the same breed that had pounded rail spikes so that men like Protestant Leland Stanford could prosper. Most of them had been victims of social prejudice. 'Irish need not apply' signs were still visible in the America of the 1920s." In 1928, Alfred E. Smith lost the presidency to Stanford graduate Herbert Hoover largely because of his Catholic faith, his immigrant origins and his opposition to Prohibition. "Saint Mary's, the school of the poor white ethnics, vented a bit of the social frustration that had accumulated in Catholic minorities in California," Andrada claims. "Those who rooted for the Gaels had at last vicariously participated in defeating the university that symbolized big money and prestige."[120] Stanford and Saint Mary's would never meet again on the gridiron. Some say the main reason was that so many players on both sides were injured in a very rough game.

THE EVENING LAW SCHOOL

In one of his most important actions, aside from hiring Madigan, Brother Gregory established a new evening law school in the fall of 1924. The catalogue of that year set forth its origin and rationale: "The institution of a Law School at Saint Mary's College is the result of an insistent demand by friends and alumni, who recognize that power for good which the Christian Brothers may exercise upon the profession of law by guiding the student through not only the humanities but to the threshold of legal practice."[121] As the law school rapidly expanded, it asked for more space on an overcrowded campus. To provide additional classrooms and offices, as well as to obtain a tax exemption from the state government, Saint Mary's College decided in 1926 to move its high school department to the campus of Saint Joseph's Academy in Peralta Park in nearby Berkeley. At a cost of $300,000, a handsome new brick classroom building was erected on that site to house the transplanted school, which was now merged with the old academy and given the new name of Saint Mary's College High School.

SEARCHING FOR A NEW LOCATION

As early as 1907, it had become apparent to district leaders that Saint Mary's either had to move to a larger campus or face possible extinction. Twelve years later, they purchased a 255-acre tract in San Leandro near Lake Chabot and announced plans to erect on it a thirteen-building complex, in the Collegiate Tudor architectural style, along with a sixty-thousand-seat football stadium. When the campaign for $3 million in construction funds was launched on October 17, news releases proclaimed that the new Saint Mary's College would soon become Saint Mary's "University." As expected, East Bay cities promised strong financial support for the proposed new school. In late 1925, the City of Oakland offered the Christian Brothers a contribution of a half million dollars, but the campaign to raise money in San Francisco proved a disaster.

The drive's overall targeted goal was $3 million, but only $450,000 was eventually collected from throughout the state. Despite this shortfall, it would have been possible to build a scaled-down Saint Mary's University in San Leandro with these diminished campaign funds, the proceeds of the sale of the old campus, the half-million-dollar grant from Oakland and a half-million-dollar bank loan the president, Brother Gregory Mallon, had managed to negotiate. By cutting out a few buildings, a Greek theater and the football stadium, total construction costs could have been reduced to around $2 million.[122] But Brother Joseph Fenlon, the provincial, would have none of it. He told higher superiors in March 1927 that Saint Mary's could not afford even a $200,000 debt and that Brother Gregory had "lost touch" with the school's financial situation in suggesting otherwise.[123]

As it turned out, Brother Joseph harbored other reasons for opposing the San Leandro location. In 1926, he warned the American assistant that "the whole [San Leandro] region had become industrial, and houses of workmen, poor houses, were actually building up and rapidly, right around our property."[124] This was a strange objection coming from the provincial of a religious order historically dedicated to teaching the lower and middle classes, if not the very poor. Brother Joseph also opposed the San Leandro schematics because he disliked the idea of changing Saint Mary's into a sprawling university and wanted to keep it a compact college.

The chance to escape industrializing San Leandro presented itself in the spring of 1926, when officials of the Los Angeles Chamber of Commerce made a tempting offer. They promised a choice site for a new campus, maybe even in Beverly Hills, and $1 million toward construction costs if Saint Mary's agreed to relocate to Southern California. As visitor,

Brother Joseph regarded the Los Angeles proposal "as the most far-reaching question that has ever come before the District, not excepting the Latin." In the end, Saint Mary's did not move to this southern lotus land of movie stars, orange groves and perpetual sunshine. Three factors explain why. First of all, the Christian Brothers and the Special Committee in the Matter of Saint Mary's College of the Los Angeles Chamber of Commerce could not agree on the right location. Brother Joseph held out for an "inviting" site within a thirty-five-minute drive of downtown Los Angeles rather than a suburb like Inglewood or Pasadena. In the second place, the local bishop would not give his full support to a massive fundraising campaign because local Catholics had been drained dry by previous appeals for diocesan building projects. Finally, the Christian Brothers themselves were not persuaded that they would be able to collect $1 million from the general public and therefore wanted a guarantee, which the chamber of commerce declined to provide, that the drive would be underwritten.[125] By the spring of 1926, the dream of a new Saint Mary's College in Beverly Hills had vanished like a desert mirage.

In February 1927, prospects for a new campus suddenly improved when the Moraga Development Company, owned by James Irvine, offered the Christian Brothers one hundred acres of free land in western Contra Costa County. The plan was to attract thousands of homeowners to a thirteen-thousand-acre housing tract by utilizing Saint Mary's College as the magnet. Brother Joseph became clamoring champion for this latest proposal, but many brothers were opposed to moving to a remote rural location. In later years, a surveyor recalled of the proffered property: "I can remember when all that was there were a few acres of farm crops, a railroad siding, horses, lizards, and some crows circling in the sky."[126] Nonetheless, in mid-March, the visitor called a special meeting of senior brothers at the Old Brickpile in Oakland to decide whether or not to move the college to a boondocks junction called Moraga.

The tactics the visitor employed in persuading the brothers to accept the Irvine offer were deceptive, perhaps even dishonest, according to the recollections of Brother Josephus Mangan. "The movement seemed to be for San Leandro" when out of the blue the visitor called leading Brothers to the Old Brickpile, ostensibly for a lecture on mathematics from a Berkeley savant. The "innocents" did not realize that the real purpose of the meeting was to hear "a discourse on the Wonders of the Moraga Valley." After a proper sales pitch, the brothers were "hustled off to 40th and Shafter," where they boarded a special Sacramento Northern trolley, which transported them to the Moraga site. After depositing its passengers, it moved to a siding at Burton Landing to clear the tracks, with only Brother Vivian Melody on board. Adamantly in favor of San Leandro, he had refused to disembark. The other brothers proceeded to wander, waist deep in hay, around a large field to get a feel for the place. The proposed site looked very much like an undeveloped "subdivision miles away from anything habitable,"[127] Brother Josephus later wrote. Flabbergasted by standing water covering the railroad tracks, Brother Gregory took the first available train back to Oakland without waiting for his confreres.[128]

Later, the other brothers returned to the Old Brickpile and waited for words from the visitor.[129] Exercising his prerogative as provincial, Brother Joseph spoke first and last and at length. There are no extant minutes of the meeting that might have recorded the contents of his speeches, but it is likely that he argued that Saint Mary's could be built in Moraga without going into debt. The land was a gift, and construction costs could be covered by the sale of the Oakland campus, the projected San Leandro campus and some property the district owned in San Mateo.[130]

After making this financial argument or something very much like it, the visitor asked for a "vote of confidence." As was customary with the brothers, "it was a white bean and black bean vote," white standing for yes and black for no. "We cast them," Brother Josephus later recalled, "[but] too many blacks appeared and the whole was swooped up and the vote was declared unanimously white." At least six prominent brothers, it would appear, favored the original San Leandro location and voted against Moraga. Brother Vivian had publically stated that we "should stick to the San Leandro site if we have to move...In San Leandro we would be in the middle of a number of growing towns and right across the Bay from growing San Mateo County." Two former Saint Mary's presidents, the director of the collegiate scholasticate, the principal of Christian Brothers High School in Sacramento and Brother Josephus also opposed the move to Moraga.[131] "Despite the opposition," Brother Matthew McDevitt writes, "Brother Joseph used his power as provincial to ride roughshod over opponents and announce through the press [that] St. Mary's College...will rise on a site in Moraga Valley, Contra Costa County instead of San Leandro and will be ready for occupancy by September, 1928."[132]

BROTHER JOSEPH FENLON'S DREAM

On May 15, 1927, the feast day of Saint John Baptist De La Salle, ground was broken for the new campus. A crowd of five thousand assembled for the ceremony, which was led by Archbishop Hanna of San Francisco. Soon the new campus began taking shape on a four-hundred-acre piece of property, the brothers having purchased an additional three hundred acres from the land company for the bargain basement price of $36,000.

Brother Joseph's plan to build the new school without going into debt proved a pipe dream. The visitor did succeed in selling the "Old Brickpile" for $850,000, which was $200,000 more than it was appraised for. However, it would appear that buyers could not be found for either the San Leandro or San Mateo properties; in 1937, Saint Mary's still listed both parcels among its assets. Short of funds, the college was forced to put up for sale, through Dean Witter Company, $1,500,000 in interest-bearing bonds to finance construction of the new buildings. Earlier, as we noted, Brother Joseph had criticized Brother Gregory for proposing to contract a $500,000 loan to build the San Leandro campus. "[O]ur ambition," Brother Joseph

The groundbreaking ceremony for the Moraga campus on May 15, 1927. *Courtesy of the Saint Mary's College Archives, Moraga.*

stated in March 1927, "is to start both institutions (Saint Mary's College and Saint Mary's College High School) off without a cent of debt." One wonders why Brother Joseph, contrary to his repeated warnings, engaged in such massive deficit financing. Eventually, the total cost of the new campus would climb to $2 million, which was about $500,000 more than had been budgeted, even though two projected buildings, an exceptionally handsome theater (auditorium) and a library, were scratched from the plans. In a letter to higher superiors, Brother Joseph did acknowledge that the anticipated sale prices for real estate holdings might not materialize and that there might be some cost overruns during construction, but he mentioned these matters only in passing without assigning them their proper weight and significance.[133] Perhaps the visitor anticipated that a larger enrollment at the Moraga campus and increased football revenues would enable the college to pay off its bondholders without too much trouble. But then the Great Depression hit.

After relinquishing the visitorship in 1927, Brother Joseph took charge of overseeing the construction of the new Moraga campus. For the sixteen months following the groundbreaking ceremony, he would act as the troubleshooter on site, living in a shack near where the old college garages were once located. For seemingly endless hours, he pored over revised blueprints, fretted over delays caused by heavy rains that made it difficult to place utility lines in the "tenacious" adobe soil and worried most of all about financing problems when the money inevitably ran out.[134]

Even before the Moraga location was selected, Brother Joseph had radically altered both the campus layout and the architectural style of the new Saint Mary's College. He had never liked the original plans for the San Leandro plant. "The buildings to me," he told the American assistant, "resembled a huge series of garages, scattered about without much reason, and almost, it would seem fortuitously. The idea…was to ape some big university." The chapel, which should have been the centerpiece, in his view, was instead "thrown back among the student dormitories." Moreover, the overall design, the visitor judged, was marred by duplication and inconvenience. With the help of a "friendly architect," Brother Joseph himself "personally dictated" the lineaments of the new plan and in such a manner as "to bring out a symbolic meaning to the school." The chapel would be in the center, flanked by buildings devoted to science and the arts.[135]

Additionally, Brother Joseph decided to abandon the Collegiate Tudor architectural style favored by Brother Gregory. He preferred a Spanish Renaissance design, augmented by touches from the Franciscan Missions of Old California. The inspiration for this change probably came from two different sources. The first was the graceful architecture of the 1915–17 Panama-California Exposition held in San Diego's Balboa Park, and the second was the early history and cultural heritage of Contra Costa County, once the home of Spanish explorer Jose Joaquin Moraga, whose adobe was located near the college site.

In fact, the Spanish Renaissance–California Mission architecture of the new campus was a brilliant choice, especially as it was realized by architect John J. Donovan. As Brother Joseph had wanted, the campus was dominated by an ornate bell tower, modeled after the cathedral in Guernavaca, Mexico, and topped by a delicate mosaic dome. On both sides of the thick-walled church, students and teachers could pause for a moment of refreshment in Mission-like flowered patios with a bubbling fountain and a wishing well. An architectural critic would later suggest that Saint Mary's College was the reincarnation of the mission world and spirit in modern times.[136]

On August 5, 1928, the new campus was formally dedicated before a crowd estimated at over ten thousand. Brother Joseph Fenlon delivered the major address of the day. He based his remarks on the noble idea that a beautiful learning environment was of paramount importance in education. "The divinely commissioned church," he went on to say, "has ever realized fully that a material object may impart an inspiring

The laying of the cornerstone at Moraga during construction. *Courtesy of the Saint Mary's College Archives, Moraga.*

lesson." With this "pedagogical principle" in mind, the visitor declared, "the Brothers of Saint Mary's set about the selection of a site that might become a veritable thing of beauty, even of grandeur, for the students destined to their care."[137]

BROTHER JOSEPH'S BREAKDOWN AND DEPARTURE

Less than seven months after the dedication of the new Saint Mary's College, the *Collegian* announced in February 1929 that Brother Joseph was going on a year's leave of absence. "Due to the terrific mental and physical strain," the article stated, "which comes of having to finish the project in the shortest time possible, with very limited funds, Brother Joseph is suffering a nervous breakdown." Plans called for sending him to a sanitarium in San Diego for

Brother Joseph Fenlon, the builder of Saint Mary's in Moraga. *Courtesy of the Christian Brothers Archives, Napa.*

a month's treatment and then on to Europe for a well-deserved vacation.[138] However, his health was too precarious to permit extensive travel. For most of 1929, he spent time in hospitals and clinics in Southern California and then went back East for some scholarly rest at the New York District novitiate in Pocantico Hills near the Rockefeller mansion in Sleepy Hollow country. Brother Joseph did not receive a warm welcome in the New York District, and he suffered a relapse just before Christmas 1929. Concluding that both his mental and spiritual health were at stake, he decided on the advice of his doctor and his confessor to ask for a dispensation from his religious vows.[139] In May 1930, he signed the official papers sent from the motherhouse in Belgium.

Ex-Brother Joseph may have become the victim of his own considerable talents. He is to be commended for awakening a province that had lain dormant for so long and for establishing the district's first collegiate house of studies. But his desire to build and progress may have overpowered his good judgment and his sense of fair play. One hardly knows whether to admire or to censure the man for what he envisioned and for what he accomplished. Both reactions would seem appropriate. It is ironic, perhaps, that one of the most capable, energetic and visionary provincials in the entire history of the San Francisco District would be the only one to forsake the institute. Although he may have left as a tarnished knight, he bequeathed a grand legacy to the province—the strikingly attractive campus of Saint Mary's College nestled in the rolling hills of Moraga. Had the college remained in Oakland, confined to a constricted campus in an outdated and ugly building, it probably would have eventually faded and folded. Somewhat grandiloquently yet truthfully, the school yearbook declared in 1928: "When any great work is completed, when a bridge is thrown across a bay, or a towering cathedral is raised into the sky, there is usually one man behind the bustle and the noise of construction who has been big enough to dream his dream and great enough to see that it has been realized. Such a man is Brother Joseph…"[140]

Chapter 7

The Golden Age

·······························

A Cathedral College in the European Tradition,
1928–1934

When the new Saint Mary's College opened in the fall of 1928, it welcomed its largest freshman class in history. Those of its students who made the transition from Oakland to Moraga were more than delighted with the new campus; one of them later exclaimed, "What a change for the better!"[141] Nonetheless, during the early years, the new Saint Mary's was a rather primitive place—isolated, barren and unadorned. An alumnus recalled that "there were no paved roads, no paved paths, no trees, no lawns. When it rained, it was all mud."[142] Students were sometimes forced to slog to class in rubber boots. Notwithstanding these primitive conditions, the first six years at the bucolic campus, roughly from 1928 to 1934, are rightly regarded as the college's "golden age."

BROTHER LEO MEEHAN, CHANCELLOR

In 1930, Brother Leo replaced Brother Lewis Treacy as president but chose the new title of "chancellor," an academic designation from medieval times. To mark Brother Leo's inauguration, the alumni and friends of Saint Mary's accorded him a grand testimonial dinner at the luxurious Palace Hotel in San Francisco, with Archbishop Edward J. Hanna and governor-elect "Sunny Jim" Rolph both in attendance.

Physically speaking, Brother Leo was a strikingly handsome man—tall, just over six feet in height, and broad shouldered; with jet black, wavy hair; a ruddy, healthy complexion; piercing eyes; "eyebrows slightly fuller than normal"; a square, strong jaw; and thin lips.[143] He was blessed, in short, with dark Irish good looks. But his most mesmerizing feature was his voice. Similar to an opera singer, Brother Leo had been born with resonant vocal chords. However, he also took pains to develop them by special breathing exercises and by talking over the ocean's roar as he walked along the shoreline.

Brother Leo Meehan, chancellor of Saint Mary's College. *Courtesy of the Saint Mary's College Archives, Moraga.*

As a speaker, Brother Leo's appeal was extremely broad—brawny college football players hung on his every word, as did the blue-rinse ladies of local women's clubs. Even those who hated poetry were instantly converted at the first sound of his mellifluous voice. He was able to tickle the funny bone at one moment and melt the heart at the next. A master of ethnic accents, Brother Leo was never affected or histrionic.

In 1939, Brother Leo substituted for Monsignor Fulton J. Sheen for a month on NBC's nationally broadcast *The Catholic Hour*. His topic was "The Catholic Tradition in Literature." One of his former students later declared that Sheen "couldn't carry Brother Leo's notes."[144] But this was not a valid comparison because Brother Leo never used prompts, even when speaking on the radio. A confrere later recalled witnessing this extraordinary ability up close during a radio broadcast in 1935. As radio programs are, this one was scheduled down to the last second. When the station engineers noticed that Brother Leo, who was speaking extemporaneously, had his eyes closed, they became visibly agitated. However, just as he reached the allotted time limit, he opened his eyes and "pronounced his final syllable." Breathless onlookers were astonished.[145]

Thousands of Brother Leo's adoring fans regularly packed into the San Francisco Opera House, the Oakland Auditorium, the Veterans' Memorial Theater and Dreamland Auditorium in San Francisco to attend his famous "Literary and Dramatic Recitals," which also featured instrumental and vocal soloists. On two nights a week during the 1930s, Brother Leo taught twin extension courses on literature for the University of California on both sides of the bay. In San Francisco, he would fill the Extension Auditorium on Powell Street to capacity and in Berkeley, either Wheeler Hall (1,400 seats) or the auditorium in the Life Sciences Building (500 seats). His students would clap wildly not only after but also during his stimulating lectures. With his evocative hand movements, perfect diction, masculine voice and dramatic acting skills, he raised lecturing to a high art.

In addition to being a gifted speaker, Brother Leo was also a prolific author. He began writing for the *San Francisco Monitor* in January 1908. In 1910, two years after Brother Leo joined the English Department at Saint Mary's, Macmillan Company asked him to edit a new version of Thomas à Kempis's classic *The Imitation of Christ*. Five years later, Brother Leo published his first book, *Contrast in Shakespeare's Historical Plays*, based on the dissertation he submitted in that year to the Catholic University of America. In 1921, he wrote a short but literate biography of Saint John Baptist De La Salle for the use of high school students. Two years later, Brother Leo authored both *Teaching the Drama and the Essay* for secondary school drama coaches and *Religion and the Study of Literature*, which was one of the favorite themes in his upper-division English courses. His only novel, *False Gods*, about an idealistic newspaper reporter who later becomes disillusioned with journalism, appeared in 1924, but it was not a critical success, and he never wrote another. In contrast, his textbook on English literature, published by Ginn and Company in 1928, was immensely popular and widely used by Catholic colleges and universities across the nation. One of the publication reviewers, probably a Harvard professor, wrote of the book, "The style is racy, breezy, arresting, and entertaining."[146]

Brother Leo Meehan's Dream: A Cathedral College in the European Tradition

When Saint Mary's moved to Moraga in the fall of 1928, it severed its ties with the evening law school. Students from the East Bay could not be expected to drive to the remote rural campus over hazardous mountain roads late at night. A year later, the college began phasing out the School of Engineering, completing the process in 1931. When named chancellor, Brother Leo warmly welcomed this "liberalization" of the college's curriculum. For him, the liberal arts provided a pathway to a rich, individuated and liberating life, notwithstanding their origins in an ancient society based on slavery. "The studies which best contribute to spiritual freedom, which will effect deliverance from the pit of ignorance, have been called the liberal arts," he once wrote.[147] In 1932, Brother Leo decided to name the twin academic buildings flanking the chapel Dante and Galileo Halls to underscore the school's commitment to the cultural values of Western civilization.

During the "golden age," Saint Mary's assumed the look and feel of a traditional English academic community. As a student of the time later wistfully recalled:

> *In the evening after dinner,* [Brother] *Leo at the head, a long line (2s) of black robed Brothers would head down toward the lake* [on campus], *a bracing walk before retiring to their studies. It created an atmosphere found everywhere in Europe on campus; particularly seen at Cambridge and Oxford over the centuries when the Dons would stroll past or run past, gowns streaming behind them as they raced to class.*[148]

The lake to which he referred, named after Saint La Salle, was actually a reservoir that supplied the college with water for domestic use as well as for irrigating the twenty acres of lawn that were eventually sodded. During the '30s, Lake La Salle also served as a pleasant recreation area. A writer for the Gael yearbook of 1939 painted this beautiful picture of its scenic charms: "Lake La Salle, limpid, cool, inviting, where many an hour is whiled away is an easy jaunt around the mossy banks…a tranquil panorama of water, sky and rolling hills to soothe the weary eye escaping from the printed word."

In 1929, Saint Mary's staged its first "public academy" to commemorate the promulgation of Pope Leo XIII's encyclical *Aeterni Patris*, which sought to revive in modern times the scholastic philosophy of the medieval schoolman Saint Thomas Aquinas. This sort of scholarly festival not only enriched the school's cultural life but also enhanced its reputation for academic excellence. On a given day, friends of the college, local ecclesiastics and distinguished academics, both local and national, would converge on the picturesque rural campus to participate with students and professors in a full round of lectures, discussions, concerts, recitals and religious services

One of Brother Leo's "public academies" in the brothers' patio. *Courtesy of the Saint Mary's College Archives, Moraga.*

honoring leading figures in Roman Catholic cultural and intellectual history such as Saint Benedict, Charlemagne and Cardinal John Henry Newman. Perhaps the most memorable of these "public academies" was dedicated to Saint Augustine. It took place in the fall of 1930 before an audience of seven hundred. Occasionally, a discussion day would be centered on a great figure outside the European Catholic tradition such as the Roman poet Virgil or the American patriot George Washington. One academy was devoted to the Oxford movement within the Church of England.

In addition to sponsoring "public academies," Brother Leo also sought to place Saint Mary's in the academic limelight by publishing a scholarly journal. In 1931, the first edition of the *Moraga Quarterly* appeared. It was edited by Brother Leo and longtime lay professor Dr. James L. Hagerty. For the inaugural issue, Brother Leo penned this elegant statement of the journal's purpose:

> *With scholarship of the stolid sort this Quarterly of ours hopes to have little to do. Etiquette demands that, however much our gentlemen of learning labor in their shirt-sleeves, they put on their coats and tie, their cravats before sitting down to write for us. We need the sturdy beef of erudition; but we want it properly cooked, judiciously seasoned, even festively garnished. In silence and in secret, we may count our calories, calculate our vitamins;*

but in public we sip the wine of urbanity and the oil of gladness. In most civilized countries autumn is the vintage season. In this Moraga valley men have planted a vineyard of the mind. The sun warms the tiny globules and clean winds set the leaves awhirl. It is time to pick the grapes. So this magazine, not so big and not at all important, is a basket wherein some of the juicy clusters fall.[149]

The *Moraga Quarterly* devoted itself mostly to literary, religious, musical, philosophical, scientific and artistic topics, with occasional poems interspersed. Although very much an in-house publication, its handsome format and well-written essays made it a publication of which Saint Mary's could be justly proud. It provided several Christian Brothers with an excellent outlet for their scholarly productions.

During Brother Leo's term as chancellor, Saint Mary's College became a renowned center of liturgical music in the western United States, through the dedicated work of the Reverend Jean M. Ribeyron. The Abbé, as he was commonly called, came to the school in 1926 to teach French for a single year but ended up living on campus for a quarter century. In the '30s, Ribeyron helped to produce two brilliant "public academies" honoring the noted Catholic polyphonic composers Tommaso Ludovico da Vittoria and Giovanni Pierluigi da Palestrina.

In the summer of 1930, an alumni group toured cultural sites throughout Western Europe. At the same time, the college offered its first summer school program; in its second year of operation, women were admitted to classes in various fields, ranging from genetics to Elizabethan literature. In addition to underwriting two distinguished lecture series, the College Alumni Association also produced an annual radio program, *Universal Saint Mary's Night,* that was beamed over a radio network throughout the western United States, from the Pacific Coast all the way to Denver in the Rockies. The first program on December 29, 1932, featured vocal and instrumental numbers, as well as remarks by Brother Leo and the president of the Alumni Association. The annual radio broadcast continued into the 1950s.

During his years as chancellor, Brother Leo continued to teach his required undergraduate course on "The Art of Study," also called Philosophy 1a. It provided an introduction to college, featuring lectures on how to study, how to prepare for a test and how to read a book, with generous doses of popular psychology and personal philosophy thrown in. The latter-day recollections of Brother Leo's numerous students afford a glimpse into the content of this course and the remarkable impact it had on them. One of Brother

Leo's favorite sayings was penned by the Roman playwright Terence: "I am human; therefore, nothing human can ever be alien to me." Brother Leo fervently embraced this catholic idea and built much of his teaching and personal life around it. He wanted his students, he often told them, to be "tolerant of people who held beliefs other than their own"; to savor the higher things of life, especially good books and good conversation; "to rarely affirm, seldom deny, and always qualify"; "to know everything about something and something about everything"; and to recognize and yield always and everywhere to what was True, Beautiful and Good. If Brother Leo's books and essays are indicative, he did much more than conjure catchy phrases or indulge in memorable aphorisms, as this list of favorite phrases recalled by his former students may lead one to believe. His

Brother Leo Meehan and Brother Agnon McCann in theatrical costumes. *Courtesy of the Christian Brothers Archives, Napa.*

published works are all elegantly written and larded with powerful literary allusions and thoughtful musings about the deeper purposes of a life well lived, the pathway to personal peace and the joys of reading. "Learned" and "graceful" are words that spring to mind after perusing Brother Leo's numerous publications.

Among the courses he taught to upper-division students were literary criticism, Dante and Shakespeare. Perhaps his most popular upper-division course was "Backgrounds of English Literature." Having traveled widely in Western Europe during a sabbatical year in 1924–25, he would paint for his students vivid pictures of the "scenic, social, historical, and religious settings" of great works of literature.[150] The first semester was devoted to a kind of literary travelogue of Italy, France and Switzerland and the second to a similar excursion to Great Britain, Ireland and Germany. One of his examination questions asked students to "state the principal literary associations of the following places: Lalaham, Horton, Stoke-Poges, Chalfont St. Giles, Rugby, Windsor, Sussex."[151] In later years, alumni would make a point of visiting the places Brother Leo had vividly described for them as undergraduates.

Football Occupies the Big Tent

At the same time Brother Leo was attempting to make Saint Mary's a top-tier liberal arts college, "Slip" Madigan was trying to turn it into the Notre Dame of the West. In many respects, both men succeeded, and that caused unavoidable conflicts of interest. Despite an undefeated season in 1929, Saint Mary's did not receive a well-deserved invitation to compete in the Rose Bowl on the grounds of its having played a light schedule. Partly in reaction to this snub, Slip decided in the following year to stretch the growing practice of "inter-sectional" football games to dramatic new lengths. In 1930, he hired a Santa Fe Railroad rooters' train, soon dubbed the "world's longest traveling bar," for a two-week cross-country jaunt to play the Fordham University Rams in the Polo Grounds of New York City. If you wanted to make it big, New York City was obviously the right place to do it, and Jesuit-operated Fordham was one of the premier football schools in the East, having won its last fourteen games. This cross-country trip became an annual affair in the '30s. Everything was top drawer—the nightly cocktail hour; cuisine; sleeping compartments; side trips to Cuba, Canada and Mexico; and hotel accommodations in New York at the Waldorf Astoria.

The Galloping Gaels and Herbert Hoover in the White House in 1930. *Courtesy of the Saint Mary's College Archives, Moraga.*

Playing in Gotham City helped make the Galloping Gaels the darlings of legendary New York City sportswriters such as Grantland Rice and Damon Runyon. During one year, the game between Saint Mary's and Fordham was beamed over the combined NBC and CBS radio networks.[152]

Perhaps the greatest of these inter-sectional games with Fordham took place in 1930, the year of their inauguration. The Galloping Gaels upset the heavily favored Rams by a score of 20–12, stunning a national radio audience. President Herbert Hoover invited the victors to the White House on the way back to California. Once the Galloping Gaels reached San Francisco, they were greeted by tens of thousands of ecstatic fans along Market Street in a ticker-tape parade larger than the one accorded the "Lone Eagle" Charles Lindbergh three years earlier.[153]

In 1929, the humorist Will Rogers drawled: "We have a team out here called St. Mary's, which sounds effeminate. But they haven't lost a game since the gold rush." One can reasonably ask how a small Catholic men's college, enrolling only about five hundred students, could have achieved such stunning success as a football powerhouse in the Depression era. Sports historian Randall Andrada insightfully identifies three main factors. The first was Madigan's clever promotional schemes. He hired publicity agents to play up his teams at press conferences; plied sports reporters with their favorite bootleg gin; threw lavish press parties in New York City, to which leading celebrities were invited; and even permitted publicists to concoct

sensational stories about his football players when regular copy ran short. Among the celebrity fans of the Galloping Gaels were Babe Ruth, Errol Flynn and Ginger Rogers. Joseph Kennedy sat on the team bench on several occasions. Madigan became friends with Jimmy Hatlo, the talented cartoonist of the *San Francisco Call-Bulletin*. In his illustrations, the Saint Mary's Saint, pictured earlier as a winged player, was transformed into the mustached Señor Moraga when the college moved to Contra Costa County. Whip in hand, Señor Moraga was normally in command of the local sports "animal act" featuring dancing bears and bucking broncos. It was said that Hatlo's cartoons did more to keep Saint Mary's College in center ring than Madigan's own colorful antics, which is saying a lot.[154]

A second reason for the success of Saint Mary's College football was the Great Depression itself. The football team provided loyal fans in the Bay Area with a few hours of colorful excitement and innocent amusement when they could forget their troubles and stifle their fears, taking vicarious satisfaction in the victory of an underdog school over insuperable odds. If the little school could triumph, so could the little guy. In 1927, Saint Mary's switched its home games from fogbound Ewing Field in San Francisco to Golden Gate Park's Kezar Stadium, seating almost sixty thousand fans. Tickets for Saint Mary's games, which were scheduled on Sundays for the convenience of the Bay Area workingman, were within the means of those lucky enough to hold onto their jobs. Fans loved to watch Madigan, attired in trench coat and flowing scarf, run up and down the sidelines barking commands to his players, excoriating officials and throwing down his lucky baseball cap in a mock fit of exasperation. According to Andrada, some observers swore that the whole show had been rehearsed before the game. Saint Mary's football games were incredibly colorful affairs—Madigan attired his players in bright silk tricolor uniforms; the college organized a hundred-piece marching band outfitted in blue and red uniforms and silver military helmets; and the Gael rooting section pioneered the use of elaborate card tricks. One sportswriter declared, "The brightest shaft of light to pierce the gloom of the depression was Slip Madigan and the Galloping Gaels."[155]

The third reason why Saint Mary's drew large crowds was the avid support of Catholic ethnic groups in the Bay Area, especially the Irish and Italians, who closely identified with the college even though they had never attended classes at the Moraga campus and perhaps had not even graduated from high school. As noted earlier, the ethnic character of the college when it was located in San Francisco was distinctly Irish. During the New Deal period, this feature was brought into high relief. "Slip" Madigan and Brother Leo Meehan, despite their decided differences, were both Irishmen to the core; so were many members of the school's football team. However, Italian surnames—Brovelli, Toscani and Nichelini—began appearing more frequently in football programs during the Depression era, much to the delight of Bay Area Italian Americans, who, like their Irish neighbors, could now also personally identify with Saint Mary's teams, gab about the Gaels at Shanty Malone's pub and cheer them on to victory.[156]

In 1933, the Saint Mary's Club was founded. Its myriad members, many of Irish and Italian immigrant stock, had never attended the college but joined the organization to offer support to a plucky little school with which they could readily identify and perhaps to enjoy, at least vicariously, the amenities and traditions of collegiate life otherwise denied them. The annual campus "homecoming" of these "streetcar alumni" in 1934 featured the celebration of Mass, a band concert and a gigantic beef barbecue in Justin Grove to the far rear of the campus. As many as seven thousand would attend these popular celebrations each year.

During the early 1930s, the football rivalry between Saint Mary's and Santa Clara intensified; indeed, some observers thought it had gotten completely out of hand. The frustrated Broncos had a hard time beating Madigan and his never-say-die players in the Roaring Twenties. Finally, in 1933, for the first time in ten years, the Broncos at least did not lose, battling the Gaels to a 6–6 tie at Kezar Stadium before a rabid crowd of sixty thousand. The hard-fought game ended in a riot. Players and thousands of fans on both sides spilled onto the field and engaged in fisticuffs and other forms of mayhem. Squads of reserve policemen wielding batons were required to quell the fighting. Shaken by the violence, Father James Lyons, president of Santa Clara, decided in early December to sever, now for the second time, all athletic relations with Saint Mary's. His decision, although roundly condemned in the press, was perfectly understandable. Coincidentally, a week after the game, a mob in San Jose, including a few Santa Clara students, lynched two young men, who were accused of brutally murdering department store heir Brooke Hart, a recent graduate of the mission school.[157]

Upset by the public scandal of two brawling Catholic colleges, San Francisco archbishop Hanna insisted that Saint Mary's and Santa Clara submit their grievances to him for arbitration. "He also demanded," according to Santa Clara historian Father Gerald McKevitt, "that motion pictures of the contest whose roughness had helped precipitate the break be delivered to the chancery office for a private screening in order that accusations of foul play might be definitively resolved." Although Father Lyons resisted Hanna's efforts to patch things up between the two warring schools, the Jesuit regional superior supported reconciliation. The annual "Little Big Game" was simply too lucrative to cancel. Under intense pressure, Santa Clara's president had no choice but to accede, and the series was resumed when the provincials of both the Jesuits and Christian Brothers reached an agreement after a year of negotiations. Facetiously, Father Lyons continued to wonder if Archbishop Hanna would pick up the hospital bills of injured players, of which there were plenty on both sides.[158]

The Chancellor Resigns

Although many students, alumni and even some Christian Brothers loved the annual hoopla of the football season, they may have failed to notice that Saint Mary's was becoming more of a football factory than a seat of learning. Old wags began to joke that the white gravel SMC sign on the hill overlooking the picturesque campus really stood for "Slip Madigan's College." On December 22, 1932, after less than three years in office, Brother Leo resigned as chancellor of Saint Mary's College. The official explanation was that he wanted more time for teaching, writing and lecturing, which may well have been the case. However, Brother Matthew McDevitt believes that Brother Leo "threw in the towel" because he opposed the ambitious football program that Madigan had built up over the years. "The excitement, hubbub, and pressure that preceded, accompanied, and followed the football season," Brother Matthew maintains, "was not conducive to create the quiet, serene atmosphere for scholarly studies."[159] One of Brother Leo's students in the late 1920s and early '30s supports the notion that he was not a big supporter of intercollegiate athletics and claims that Brother Leo never attended any football games. "Athletics were prominent at the College," this alumnus told provincial archivist Brother Alfred Brousseau in 1983. But for Brother Leo, "athletics were present but not discussed in his classes." In 1931, when the football team traveled to Los Angeles to play USC, most classes were cancelled on Friday, but not Brother Leo's.[160]

One of Brother Leo's student chauffeurs, William G. "Bill" Simon, offers a different take on the chancellor's attitude toward collegiate sports. He told Andrada, "No, he was not vehemently opposed to football, no I don't think that would be a fair summation. He felt the cultural and academic aspects should just not be overshadowed by athletics."[161] The chancellor himself once wrote: "Earnest college instructors used to bewail the overemphasis on athletics in the Grove of Academe. They did not utterly condemn games and physical exercise; they merely insisted that first things should be first, that, as Woodrow Wilson once reminded the sports-mad alumni of Princeton, the side show is not the main tent."[162] The problem, according to Brother Matthew, was that football had become the "main tent" rather than the "sideshow."

In 1933, one of Professor Hagerty's former students wrote to him from Georgetown about the tug-of-war between the competing images of Saint Mary's as a seat of learning and a football factory. While noting a steady "tendency to raise the scholastic and intellectual value of the College," he confessed that "many people in the East think of the alma mater as an athletic club which is using its athletic teams to pay off the mortgage." However, "a few more accomplishments like" the *Moraga Quarterly* and the "literary pursuits of the school newspaper might remove this far too prevalent opinion,"[163] he hoped. Unfortunately, the athletic side of the college's life became even more prominent in the early '30s despite Brother Leo's best efforts. Still, he was surely the most famous and the most learned Christian Brother ever to teach at Saint Mary's College. As one of his former students rightly put it, "He was the colossus of academia in that era, and we shall never see his likes again."[164] But neither will there ever be another "Slip" Madigan.

Chapter 8
The College Declares Bankruptcy

·······································

The Presidency of Brother Albert Rahill,
1934–1941

On July 1, 1934, Saint Mary's stopped making interest payments to its bondholders. At this point, it owed them $1,370,500 in principal and something over $200,000 in unpaid interest. Had the college not incurred such a large debt in building its new campus, it might have weathered the Great Depression without too much difficulty. However, it could not realistically hope to keep paying off its investors and balance its annual budget at the same time after the stock market crashed in 1929 and the school's enrollment began to plummet. Profits from the big-time football program, which had been pegged for bond payments, were now diverted to cover yearly operating costs.

As it turns out, much of the pigskin revenue had been wasted; in some years, the football program spent almost as much as it took. In addition, too many students had scholarships in relation to the small size of the student body. At the end of the Madigan era, only 12 students, out of 335, paid the full amount for tuition and room and board; 248 were on full or partial scholarships of one kind or the other. This speaks well of the brothers' generosity but not of their management skills. An institution built for 1,000 boarders had fewer than 300; increasing this number by a mere 100 students who paid the full freight of $750 during the mid-1930s would have basically solved the institution's financial problems.

In March 1935, Brother Albert Rahill, the principal of Saint Mary's College High School in Berkeley, was named president. At five feet, three inches, he was probably the shortest college president in the country; at thirty-five years

Brother Albert Rahill, president when the college was sold to Archbishop Mitty. *Courtesy of the Christian Brothers Archives, Napa.*

of age, he was probably the youngest; with only two years of college, he was probably the least credentialed. "So a great deal of noise was made about this trivial circumstance [of his young age]," his confrere and colleague Brother Albert Brousseau claims. Brother Albert even appeared on the popular *Rudy Vallee* radio show. The "PR challenge" was to deflect attention from his lack of a BA degree. The University of San Francisco graciously came to the rescue by granting Brother Albert an honorary doctorate the year he became president. The whole thing had been "engineered."[165] (Brother Alfred's critical comments about Brother Albert's sparse academic credentials should be placed in context. In 1937, Brother Alfred became the first Christian Brother in the San Francisco District to earn a bona fide PhD. It was in advanced physics, and two of his professors were J. Robert Oppenheimer and Ernest Orlando Lawrence. Later, as provincial, Brother Alfred urged all of his confreres to acquire their BA degree and sent several

Brother Alfred Brousseau, the first college brother to earn a PhD. *Courtesy of the Christian Brothers Archives, Napa.*

of them to leading universities for advanced degrees. Brother Albert's lack of academic enterprise clearly bothered him.)

When Brother Albert took up the reins of office in 1935, he must have realized he would be in for a very bumpy ride. As he explained to a New York City reporter, "I was the goat. I guess they didn't have anybody else to make president, so they picked on me."[166] Not "picked me" but "picked *on* me," as if a bully had come down hard on a defenseless little guy. It must have taken more than a little courage for the newly appointed president, without a bachelor's degree or any previous collegiate administrative experience, to assume the leadership of a bankrupt school facing such formidable financial problems. One must admire his moxie and his sense of obedience.

The Road to Foreclosure and Sale

The college's best hope was to prolong the current condition of default until such a time as it could resume interest payments or negotiate a new agreement with its creditors. In the fall of 1935, the bondholders succeeded in persuading the state corporation commissioner to reorganize the college's financial management under the threat of foreclosure. With the concurrence of Brother Albert, James Everett Butler was appointed the college's comptroller but was subsequently removed from office when he attempted to trim the pigskin program. The bondholders organizing committee was furious. To add insult to injury, late in 1936, Brother Albert gave "Slip" Madigan most of the Fordham game profits, amounting to more than $36,000, for unpaid back "gate commissions." Considering the coach a general creditor among other general creditors, the bondholders' committee decided to foreclose on the college. It was also upset by the college's failure to attract more students or set up an endowment fund.

On July 25, 1937, a sweltering summer day later dubbed "Black Friday," a crowd of about forty reporters, photographers and "news hawks" gathered on the steps of the Alameda County Courthouse to witness the auction of the college to the highest bidder. The bespectacled trust officer of the Central Bank of Oakland took almost fifty minutes to read, in "a low drone," the long bill of sale. After fifteen minutes, the crowd had dwindled to a handful. A street "urchin" hit up the remnant for nickels but pocketed only one. At last, the bank officer opened up the bidding, offering at auction not only the Moraga campus but also, in turn and separately, three additional properties belonging to the college: the campus of the high school in Berkeley, 247 unimproved acres on Foothill Boulevard in San Leandro and 47 unimproved acres in the city of San Mateo. "Do I hear any bid for Parcel No. 1?" he asked. There was complete silence; it continued as other offers were made. Heightening the drama, a long funeral procession wound down the adjoining street. "Do I hear," the auctioneer continued, wiping sweat from his brow, "any bid for the properties of St. Mary's College in their entirety?" Two mustached "mystery men" in panama hats put in a bid of $411,150. They were the attorneys of a prominent San Francisco law firm that had been representing the bondholders. A correspondent from *Time* magazine later reported that as cameras clicked, they passed the trust officer "a crumpled cashier's check of $43,000. Thus transferred lock, stock & barrel...was the most famed little football college on the West Coast."[167] Photographs of both buyers, along with one of the campus, appeared in the August 9 edition of *Life* magazine. The sale of the college had become a national news story.

Immediately after the sale of the college, negotiations commenced between Archbishop John J. Mitty of San Francisco and the law offices of Pillsbury, Madison and Sutro either to lease or purchase Saint Mary's. The bondholders were only interested in an immediate cash sale so they could quickly recoup as much of their original investments as possible. For the Christian Brothers, the clock was ticking ominously. If a deal was not struck, the students at the college in Moraga and its high school in Berkeley would face eviction at the beginning of the fall semester. In the nick of time, on September 17, 1937, Mitty purchased both institutions for $715,000. Three days later, he told the apostolic delegate in Washington "that this has been the best possible solution to a very unsavory financial episode and that the Brothers will be able to carry on their work."[168] Now that the archbishop owned the college, he insisted that Madigan's 10 percent of gate receipts be rescinded, and it was.

Once the college was saved from closing, Brother Albert embarked on a long-overdue campaign to raise the money to buy it back. Brother Leo lent his beautiful voice to the effort. Under the sponsorship of the college's recently established Ladies' Guild, he gave without a fee a series of Lenten Lectures at the War Memorial Opera House in San Francisco in 1938. Tickets were a hefty three dollars.

The Diamond Jubilee

Archbishop Mitty's purchase of Saint Mary's was fortuitous. "Coming as it does, at the beginning of our Diamond Jubilee year, we are very hopeful for the future," Brother Albert declared in September 1937. "Relieved of the financial burden and worries concerning the future of the College, we now have something upon which to build. With the existence of the College assured, I look forward to the coming year with great optimism."[169] On May 15, the feast of Saint John Baptist De La Salle, the diamond anniversary commencement ceremony was held on campus. Monsignor Peter Guilday, the president of the Catholic University of America, delivered the major address of the day. He told the graduates:

> *The basic principles of Christian citizenship—right thinking and right conduct—the Brothers brought to San Francisco three score and ten years ago; and in spite of many a sad and serious setback, every day of that long span has been given generously to this State for the education of its youth. Who can measure the service? What pen can describe all that the Brothers by precept and example have added to the cultural advance of this great commonwealth of the West?*[170]

The words in this address that stand out are "serious and sad" setbacks, of which there have been many in the history of Saint Mary's. Bankruptcy was surely among the worst.

In late 1938, while Saint Mary's was celebrating its seventy-fifth anniversary, Robert Maynard Hutchins, president of the University of Chicago, published a provocative article in the *Saturday Evening Post* entitled "Gate Receipts and Glory," in which he blamed football for the college's financial woes. Declaiming that "athleticism, like crime, does not pay," he noted that "last summer St. Mary's College, home of the Galloping Gaels, was sold at auction and bought in by a bondholders' committee. This was the country's most sensational football college. Since 1924 it has won eighty-six and tied seven of its 114 games." Despite "inexpensive" academic efforts and "immense" gate receipts, the institution still went bankrupt. "The bondholders were surprised to learn it was running $72,000 a year behind its budget. They were even more surprised to learn that football expenses were almost equal to football income." However, as the president of a major university with a big-time football program, Hutchins was not. He knew that "to make big money in athletics you have to spend big money" on stadiums, equipment, coaches salaries, travel expenses and publicity, which is exactly what Madigan did.[171]

"SLIP" MADIGAN IS FIRED

On March 11, 1940, Saint Mary's College issued the following press release:

> *J. Philip Murphy, chairman of the Board of Athletic Control…announced today that the board had decided not to renew Mr. Edward P. ("Slip") Madigan's contract, which will expire on March 31, 1941. Murphy stated that Norman P. ("Red") Strader would handle the football squad in this year's Spring training but added that Madigan's salary rights under the contract would be respected even though Mr. Madigan will have no jurisdiction over the balance of the 1940 Spring training or the 1940 regular season.[172]*

In short, after nineteen years as head coach of the Galloping Gaels, the legendary "Slip" Madigan, perhaps America's most famous football coach since Knute Rockne, had been "unceremoniously bounced" by the college administration.[173] Although rumors had been circulating about "Slip's" declining health and a possible move to another college or even to the pros, the revelation of his firing came as a terrific shock to football fans across the nation. The dazed student body president of the college told a reporter of the *San Francisco Chronicle*: "St. Mary's without Madigan would be like St. Mary's without the chapel."[174]

If left to his own devices, Brother Albert probably would not have fired Madigan. Both men were public personalities cut from the same colorful Irish cloth. In addition, Brother Albert was a strong supporter of intercollegiate

"Slip" Madigan on the practice field in his business suit. *Courtesy of the Saint Mary's College Archives, Moraga.*

football, unlike President Hutchins, and seems to have thoroughly enjoyed all the glamour and glitz of the Madigan era. A newspaper article in 1935 reported that Brother Albert "is the first college head in memory of St. Mary's alumni who made a practice of entering the football players' locker room before games to hearten the team with friendly slaps on shoulders and words of encouragement. Of himself he said: 'I'm a very modern type of individual. I enjoy a good, clean show. I get a real kick out of life. Why be pessimistic?'"[175] The president seems merely to have acquiesced in the board's brave decision. At the time of Madigan's dismissal, he declared, "The Board felt they needed a change and I listened to them…That's when I said yes."[176]

The time for a change had surely come. The coach's salary was too large, and football had come to dominate the school, threatening its academic and even its moral health. There is no indication that Madigan was a dishonest man, as some have charged; however, he was clearly benefitting more from the big-time football program than was the bankrupt college. Slip negotiated a deal with St. Mary's for a severance package of $14,000. This settlement was quite generous considering the school's financial plight. Now Saint Mary's would have to pay a total $21,000 for two football coaches.

After leaving Saint Mary's, Madigan pursued a successful career in business. He died in Oakland on October 10, 1966, shortly before being reconciled to Brother Albert. The two men had arranged for a peacemaking luncheon date for the twelfth, unfortunately two days after Slip had passed. At the wake, Madigan's son Eddie reminded Brother Albert of the engagement they had made for the morrow. Later, Brother Albert reminisced: "I think I prayed the better for Slip that night thinking of the date…I loved Slip. I will never forget him. I go on record in gratitude…He is one gentleman who has made a great contribution to Saint Mary's College."[177]

Hollywood Tells the Saint Mary's Story

The saga of Saint Mary's triumphs on the gridiron, its bankruptcy, its purchase by the archbishop and Madigan's firing was too melodramatic to escape the notice of Hollywood. In 1953, John Wayne, Donna Reed and Charles Coburn starred in the movie *Trouble Along the Way*, a thinly veiled account of the college's travails in the 1930s. Although a romantic comedy, in which a divorced father fights for the custody of his young daughter, the main plot revolves around the attempt of a tiny Catholic college (referred to as "bankruptcy university") to keep from closing by fielding a lucrative football team under a new coach. Salvation through gate receipts! Saint Mary's College becomes Saint Anthony's College and is transferred from rural Contra Costa County to an urban setting in New York City. The Christian Brothers' congregation becomes an order of religious priests attired in cassocks, capes and birettas. (They look suspiciously like Jesuits!) Finally, Edward Patrick "Slip" Madigan becomes Stephen "Steve" Aloysius Williams, the character played by John Wayne.

The first potential new coach contacted by Saint Anthony's (a man named "Buck" Holman, perhaps after Lawrence "Buck" Shaw of Santa Clara) demands a salary of $25,000, far too much for the struggling school, but Williams, who has been surviving as a sports bookie, settles for a more modest $3,000. He explains to Father Matthew William Burke, the rector of Saint Anthony's, played by crusty character actor Charles Coburn, that it would take four years to build up a good football team and to arrange a schedule of major opponents, but time is of the essence. The local provincial wants to close the school at the end of the coming semester because he can't abide an accumulated debt of $170,000. A big part of the financial problem is that 85 percent of the students are not paying full tuition. With the direct intervention of the local cardinal, William Patrick O'Shea, a top-notch football schedule is quickly put together, including real Catholic football powers such as Holy Cross, Villanova and Notre Dame, as well as a fictional school called Santa Carla (read Santa Clara), dubbed the top Catholic football college on the West Coast. Given a "free hand," Williams recruits "players" by forging records and scouring coal mines, stages illegal summer practices and lures assistant coaches by promising them a cut of the profits. In their first game under the new coach, the football team beats the Santa Carla Lions (read Broncos) 28–0, before a packed crowd in the Polo Grounds, where Saint Mary's used to play Fordham. Seeking revenge because of a custody fight, the coach's ex-wife informs the school's president of the coach's shady practices. He is dismissed, and the remainder of the schedule is cancelled. "You are destroying the things the school stands for," the rector tells Williams.

All is not lost, however. The cardinal, a graduate of the school, prevails on the provincial to continue subsidizing Saint Anthony's, and its doors remain open. An ecclesiastical assistant demands that Saint Anthony's watch its pennies and increase revenue by establishing a School of Commerce, but the rector rejects a pecuniary approach to the school's financial problems in favor of maintaining the liberal arts in their purity. The cardinal, who once studied English literature under the beloved rector, seems to concur. In the end, the rector apologizes to the coach because he had only done what had been asked of him and even extends his contract. Finally, in good Hollywood form, the John Wayne character falls in love with the attractive probation officer, played by a young Donna Reed, who is attempting to take away his daughter, although their eventual marriage is only hinted at.

A Bridge and a Tunnel

One of the biggest stories on campus during the 1930s, prominently featured in the pages of the school newspaper along with striking photos, was not about the antics of "Slip" Madigan or even the college's financial troubles but about the looming prospect that Saint Mary's would soon be pulled out of its rural isolation by a dramatic new bridge spanning the bay and a three-mile double-bore tunnel cutting through the coastal range. The headline of a *Saint Mary's Collegian* article on May 10, 1935, tells the whole story: "Bringing the College Closer to the Metropolitan Area." Ever since its establishment in Moraga in 1928, the school had suffered from the inability of East Bay students to easily commute to it. Recall that the successful law school was dropped for that very reason. Up to the late 1930s, there were basically only two means of access to Saint Mary's: the Sacramento Northern commuter rail line that stopped at a little station at the foot of the campus and the narrow, dangerous Fish Ranch Road that climbed over the coastal range down into the Moraga Valley. However, during the 1930s, two big New Deal public works projects promised to finally bring Oakland, San Francisco and other Bay Area cities into closer contact with the college. The first was the majestic Oakland–San Francisco Bay Bridge; the second was the Broadway Low Level Tunnel, now known as the Caldecott Tunnel, named after Mayor Thomas E. Caldecott of Berkeley. The first project was completed on November 12, 1936, and the second, a year later, with Brother Leo as one of the featured speakers at the dedication ceremony on December 3. Anticipating that the new bridge and tunnel would have a favorable effect on a student body decimated by the Great Depression, the college launched a publicity campaign for more day students and scheduled laboratory classes in the morning so that commuters could work in the afternoon. However, it was not until the 1960s that Saint Mary's became an integral part of the Bay Area.

Brother Albert's Presidency

Brother Albert's tenure was tumultuous because of the trying times through which he lived, the formidable challenges he faced and some of the questionable decisions he made. He can't be blamed for lacking proper academic credentials or previous collegiate experience because the decision to name him president was made by his religious superiors. Given Brother Albert's lack of a scholastic background and the huge financial troubles he faced, one would not expect great academic accomplishments during his administration. However, he did lift the science departments to the level of a school equal to liberal arts and business and establish a major in journalism, both of which were laudable achievements. However, his most "valuable contributions were not in the area of scholarship and teaching." What he did do was to use "some valuable personality qualities…to advantage for the College and the Brothers."[178] As a public relations figure, Brother Albert represented the college with dash and grace, and he was loved by the students for his accessibility and charm.

Brother Albert's socializing in smart cafés during the Depression era arched more than a few eyebrows in the Bay Area, including the archbishop's, but his "worldliness" was put to good use in defusing a potentially serious legal problem facing the bankrupt college. It seems that Madigan's overheated sports publicity office invented a story falsely accusing Hollywood movie star Jean Harlow of being romantically linked with a handsome Saint Mary's football player, named Jim Austin, who had worked on the MGM lot as a summer laborer. The studio threatened to sue Saint Mary's after a newspaper article placed the blond bombshell in a bad light. Brother Albert decided to visit Miss Harlow at her room in the Biltmore Hotel in Los Angeles to smooth ruffled feathers. At the meeting, she asked the diminutive brother if he would like some ginger ale, coffee or tea. He said, "No, thanks," to each offer in turn. A bit flustered, Jean asked, "Well, how about some scotch?" Brother Albert replied, "Why certainly." (Scotch was his favorite libation.) Shedding tears, the glamorous star confided to Brother Albert, "All this publicity I have no control over. I guess the world must think I am an old bitch." The president commiserated, and the encounter ended happily. The studio never sued Saint Mary's for the fictitious story. The last thing Saint Mary's needed was an expensive lawsuit.[179]

In assessing Brother Albert's administration, it is sometimes difficult to distinguish between appearance and reality. His good friend Brother Mel Anderson helps to explain why:

Brother Albert was placed in a vulnerable and almost untenable position by the Visitor who appointed him. He had to look good to the public, whether he liked it or not. The P.R. people were as inventive as they could be, mostly likely excessively so. But it probably did not make one iota of a difference to the public or the students who found him congenial and a man who exhibited all the trappings and eloquence that a President should have. Was he devious and cunning? Probably not. He was a good actor, but not by choice. He was as obedient as he could be and did the best he could under the circumstance.[180]

Although quite generous, this assessment is also fair-minded.

Chapter 9

Saint Mary's College in War and Peace

·······························

The Presidency of Brother Austin Crowley, 1941–1950

A fter two terms as president, Brother Albert Rahill left office in the summer of 1941; his replacement was Brother Austin Crowley. He was also a colorful Irishman but much less suave; it was said of Brother Austin that he thought a good argument was the ideal form of communication. A former student later recalled, "He replaced the very popular and extremely personable Brother Albert, and his bluntness jarred many of those who had been students under the previous administration."[181] Perhaps Brother Austin's brusque personality was not ideal for a college president, but it was exactly what Saint Mary's College needed during the turbulent war years when, once again, its very existence hung by a thread.

Brother Austin enjoys the notable distinction of being the first president to possess a bona fide PhD. In 1943, at the nearby

Brother Austin Crowley, president during World War II. *Courtesy of the Christian Brothers Archives, Napa.*

University of California, he successfully defended a 245-page dissertation on "Costumbrism in Chilean Literary Prose of the Nineteenth Century." (Costumbrism is a literary movement, on the fringes of Romanticism, focusing on the everyday life of common people and employing realistic language.) As a result of his rich and rewarding experience at Berkeley, Brother Austin maintained close ties over the years with his former distinguished professors in the Romance Languages Department.

Brother Leo Leaves the Institute

On August 22, 1941, shortly after Brother Austin took office, the *Saint Mary's Collegian* carried a short item informing the campus community that the popular professor Brother Leo Meehan was taking a leave of absence to write and travel but would return in a year.[182] Although plausible, this was really a cover story. Nine days earlier, the official papers dispensing Brother Leo from his religious vows were processed in Rome. However, it was not until October 30 that the *San Francisco Chronicle* and other dailies throughout the country reported on his "secularization" by the Vatican. Meehan's myriad admirers were greatly surprised, even shaken, that he would abandon the religious life as an older man. A confrere confessed that he would have been less shocked if Archbishop Mitty or one hundred of his priests had jumped ship.

To this day, the reasons for Brother Leo's departure are difficult to determine. Some brothers maintain that Brother Leo had accumulated $100,000 in lecture fees and book royalties and therefore could look forward to a secure and comfortable retirement.[183] Others claimed that he had become a "mundane intellectual." Perhaps because he was so attractive to women, it was rumored that a paramour was involved and that he would marry quite soon. When asked by reporters if this were true, he responded, "I want to deny unequivocally those rumors. I am not angry about them, but they are untrue." Then he added with typical wit: "As a matter of fact it is quite a compliment to be subject of a marriage rumor at my age."[184] In his last years as a lecturer, Brother Leo played on the theme of "knowing when to quit," which was in fact the title of the last column he wrote for the *San Francisco Monitor* in 1940. Perhaps conscious of his diminishing powers, Brother Leo may have wanted, as he wrote in this piece, to "drop the curtain on our little comedy while acting is still vital and the audience has not succumbed to polite boredom."[185] Of course, he could have retired while remaining a Christian Brother. So there must have been deeper reasons for his return to secular life. In his own petition for a dispensation from his vows, Meehan confided to higher superiors that he did not think that continued membership in the institute was conducive to a fruitful and productive life. He also mentioned, without going into any great detail, that he found himself out of harmony with community practices and educational procedures at Saint Mary's.[186] In fact, the religious community at Moraga during Brother Albert's administration left much to be desired. There were problems with irregularity, excessive drinking and boorish behavior,[187] not to mention the turmoil over the bankruptcy and sale of the college and the firing of "Slip" Madigan. This was not the quiet and serene atmosphere that Brother Leo was looking for in retirement.

Not long after withdrawing from the institute, Dr. Francis Meehan, as he was now called, purchased a beautiful home on the shores of Lake Sherwood in Southern California and christened it Casa Della Madonna. In 1946, Meehan married DeNeze Brown, a former restaurant hostess at the Clift Hotel in San Francisco, who was twenty-two years his junior. She had met Brother Leo years earlier as a student in one of his University of California extension courses. Ex-Brother Leo died on December 11, 1966, at the age of eighty-five in Oxnard, California. One of his former student chauffeurs, William G. "Bill" Simon, was at his bedside. The funeral was held at Old Saint Mary's in San Francisco at the entrance to Chinatown. A respectable contingent of Brother Leo's former students attended the requiem Mass; some served as pallbearers. Several had earlier made regular pilgrimages to Casa Della Madonna to sit at his feet once again. Countless more modeled their lives on his teachings and maxims, which remained dear to them for their whole lives.[188] "I am human; therefore, nothing human can ever be alien to me."

HERE COMES THE NAVY

Just as the Great Depression dominated Brother Albert's term as president, so did the Second World War color Brother Austin's. When the Empire of Japan attacked the United States on December 7, 1941, college officials feared that the school, burdened with a heavy debt and still in hock to the archbishop of San Francisco, might have to bolt its doors, as most of its all-male students went off to fight the Axis Alliance. However, the federal

Naval cadets assembled in front of the makeshift wartime college building. *Courtesy of the Saint Mary's College Archives, Moraga.*

government came to the school's rescue a few months after the United States joined the worldwide conflict. On February 27, 1942, Brother Austin received the following telegram from Secretary of the Navy Frank Knox in Washington: "St. Mary's College has been selected by the Navy Department as one of the four locations for pre-flight training. Your patriotic cooperation in this vital program is appreciated." The other schools chosen for the training program, located in different parts of the country, were the public universities of Iowa, Georgia and North Carolina.

In the negotiations between Brother Austin and Washington officials, it became clear that the navy wanted to commandeer the entire property and move the college to the Peralta Park campus of Saint Mary's College High School in Berkeley or perhaps even to the novitiate at Mont La Salle in Napa. Other possible sites were the College of Arts and Crafts in Oakland and a discarded World War I military site in Clyde beyond Concord near Suisun Bay. However, the president was strenuously opposed to any and all of these options and had been since an interview with Archbishop Mitty back in December 1941. He strongly believed that

Naval cadets marching in front of the chapel during World War II. *Courtesy of the Saint Mary's College Archives, Moraga.*

if Saint Mary's moved to an urban location, it would never return to Moraga. He was probably right.

The first cadets arrived in Moraga on June 12, 1942, and were greeted by Lieutenant Commander Clyde King, executive officer, and Captain George W. Steele, commanding officer, both of whom had been on campus since

April making extensive preparations. While stationed at Saint Mary's, the new recruits, who usually numbered around two thousand at any one time, took technical classroom courses to prepare themselves for regular flight school. However, most of their time was spent in a demanding physical "toughening" program designed by the famous boxer Gene Tunney. An article in the *Berkeley Gazette*, announcing the establishment of the new pre-flight school, noted that the naval cadets would "undergo vigorous exercises, including wood chopping, 41-mile hikes, boxing, swimming, and football."[189] From late 1944 to the spring of 1945, future president Gerald R. Ford served as an instructor and football coach in the Athletic Department, having been a star football player at the University of Michigan, but he lived in an apartment off campus in Orinda.

Existing facilities on campus could not accommodate the navy's needs, so huge frame buildings were quickly thrown up to serve as barracks, a boxing pavilion, mess halls, a sick bay and a field house. A rifle range was laid out to the rear of the campus for target practice, and perhaps the largest indoor swimming pool in the world was dug out of the campus's putty-like adobe soil. A new entrance road leading up to the chapel was cut and paved, and the bridge of the old access road near Lake La Salle was reinforced. Sewage, heating and electrical facilities were greatly expanded, and a two-

Aerial view of the campus showing the navy pre-flight school installations. *Courtesy of the Saint Mary's College Archives, Moraga.*

mile water line was dug between the college and the town of Lafayette in order to connect with the East Bay Municipal Water District. The two main academic halls were renamed for aircraft carriers.

DR. HAGERTY AND THE GREAT BOOKS PROGRAM

While naval cadets were parading around the campus, the regular college continued to function, thanks to Brother Austin's insistence, in a corner on the north side of the property in makeshift buildings. Supported by a small group of Christian Brothers, Dr. James L. Hagerty utilized the war to make Saint Mary's into a pure liberal arts college devoted to the study of the "Great Books of the World." In 1941, before the cadets arrived on campus, the first seminars based on reading and discussing classical texts in chronological order were introduced to the college as an upper-division elective, entitled Philosophy 182a–182b. In the following year, all incoming freshmen were required to take a seminar on Greek Thought and Culture, along with a fixed program consisting of English composition, a foreign language, physics, public speaking, religion and a mathematics course devoted in the first semester to the *Elements* of Euclid. The conversion of the college to a Great Books Program marks one of the more dramatic reversals in the history of American higher education—from a school that only fifteen years

Professor James L. Hagerty, who introduced the Great Books Program during World War II, with Father Charles Baschab. *Courtesy of the Saint Mary's College Archives, Moraga.*

earlier had taught mining, sewer construction, hydraulics, land surveying, the theory of trusses, tunnel construction, architecture, foreign trade, education and law to one devoted exclusively to the study of the traditional liberal arts and the careful reading of the classical texts of Western civilization. The supporters of the Great Books Program at Saint Mary's College looked upon themselves as the leaders on the West Coast of a broader movement, which had begun a few years earlier at Saint John's College in Annapolis, to renew the face of American higher education during and after the Second World War.

The novel, even radical, nature of the changes made in 1943 fomented strong opposition on campus from those Christian Brothers whose philosophy of education stressed professional and vocational preparation in fields such as engineering, commerce, law, architecture and education. The leader of this group was Brother Cornelius Braeg, a recognized expert on

Brother Cornelius Braeg speaking to a student. *Courtesy of the Saint Mary's College Archives, Moraga.*

the paintings of western landscape artist William Keith. Throughout the war years, he wrote vigorous tracts against the new Great Books Program. Among other things, Brother Cornelius argued that the Seminar Program failed to prepare students for future careers, appealed only to the brightest, encouraged students to be overly argumentative and did not place classical texts in their proper historical context.[190] Perhaps even more important, he contended that the "New Plan" was opposed to the teachings of Saint La Salle. This was always a clincher in any argument over curriculum. "St. de La Salle, if he had a choice in this case, would certainly stay with the practical program," Brother Cornelius asserted. "Did he not put Latin out of his schools to give place to the practical vernaculer [*sic*]? And did he not establish special technical courses, e.g., drafting in Sunday schools, and in a certain school special courses for tradesmen?"[191] Clearly, the basic issues involved in the Latin Question were still alive.

Football Survives on a Wing and Prayer

Although the Great Bookers succeeded in drastically revising the curriculum, they did not manage to eliminate the school's big-time football program. In 1939, President Hutchins had succeeded in abolishing football at the University of Chicago, once a prominent member of what became the Big Ten Conference. After the United States entered the Second World War, many colleges across the nation dropped intercollegiate football for lack of students, players and resources. However, Saint Mary's officials decided to retain its pigskin program in order to maintain "a sense of normalcy" during the war emergency, keep up enrollment and reinforce student morale on a campus "flooded" with naval cadets.[192] Teams composed mostly of freshmen and military rejects kept Saint Mary's on the gridiron in 1943 and 1944, but only barely. Against the University of Southern California in 1944, coach Jimmy Phelan was forced to play both a sixteen-year-old boy with a withered hand and an epileptic.

With enrollment drastically reduced, Saint Mary's officials gave serious consideration to dropping football after the team lost all five scheduled games during the 1944 season. However, a group of talented athletes arrived on campus in the fall of 1945, the financial picture brightened and plans to eliminate football were shelved. The happy-go-lucky football team, stocked with exceptionally young players, would sometimes sing unabashedly in the

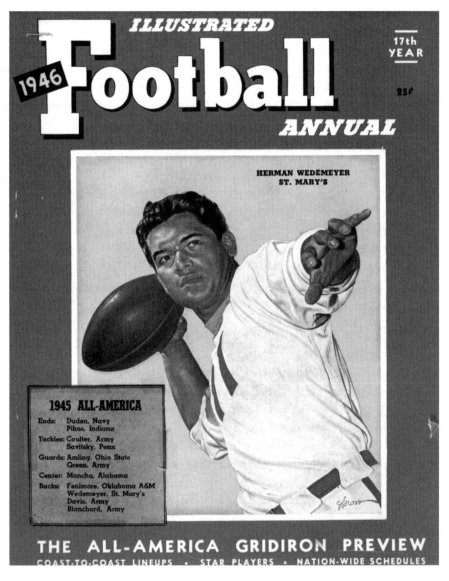

Herman Wedemeyer on the cover of a football magazine. *Courtesy of the Saint Mary's College Archives, Moraga.*

huddle before calling a play, prompting the nickname the "Singing Saints." According to Andrada, these carefree youngsters "laughed" and "sang" their way from one victory to another. Only once, when they played the College of the Pacific in Stockton, did they seem "awe-struck." Although the Galloping Gaels trampled the Tigers, 61–0, after the game team members lined up to humbly introduce themselves to Pacific's coach, Amos Alonzo Stagg. "There was little pleasure in embarrassing a living legend and a boyhood idol," Andrada comments.[193]

The acknowledged star of the Galloping Gaels was strikingly handsome "Squirmin" Herman Wedemeyer from Hawaii; versatile as a player, he could run, pass and punt with equal skill. The darling of teenage girls across the country, Wedemeyer later became a featured actor on the 1970s television program *Hawaii Five-O*. A heart attack dashed his plans to run for governor of Hawaii. However, he did become an accomplished golfer and landscape painter. After achieving a national ranking during the 1945 season, the Galloping Gaels were invited to play Oklahoma A&M in the Sugar Bowl in New Orleans on January 1, 1946. Despite a Gael loss, the "Whiz Kids," as team members were also called, remained the clear favorites of sportswriters throughout the nation.

THE NAVY LOWERS ITS FLAGS

Beginning in 1945, Brother Austin began negotiating with the United States Navy for its impending evacuation from campus. The tone of his letters to federal authorities was always polite and proper but also very tough-minded. He told them that Saint Mary's College had been happy to help in the war effort and even to make patriotic sacrifices for the Allied cause, but he was also determined to uphold and protect the institution's legitimate rights. In February of the year the war finally ended, the president informed Commander Gerard Swope Jr., counsel of the Bureau of Naval Personnel, that "insofar as a purchase of St. Mary's property, by the Government, is concerned, St. Mary is not, and will not be, interested in a voluntary sale; it plans to resume its college operations, in full measure, here as soon as the Government surrenders possession of its campus properties." Brother Austin informed Swope that the college was not interested in retaining the temporary buildings the navy had erected because it had no use for them. Even while expressing his willingness to pay for any improvements Saint Mary's wanted to retain, he insisted on compensation from the government for any damages that had been done to the school's property and buildings.[194] In May 1946, the navy hauled down its flags and left the campus.

Dismantling the Wartime Curriculum

During the postwar years, Brother Austin's most significant action was to dismantle many of the educational reforms that had been enacted during World War II. It was originally expected that the new Great Books Program would be retained after the "duration." An article in the *Berkeley Gazette*, quoting Brother Austin, reported on February 27, 1942: "It is quite probable that the College may be put into operation on a new teaching policy, allowing for a much more extended use of the seminar and tutorial methods with a view to the complete adoption of such a policy on the return of normal conditions." However, the total curricular transformation begun in 1942 did not survive the postwar period, basically for two reasons. To generate revenue to buy back the college from Archbishop Mitty, Brother Austin decided to restart its lucrative big-time football program. The Great Books and football players don't mix very well. His second reason for opening up the curriculum was to meet the needs of returning veterans who were flocking to Saint Mary's and other colleges and universities. Generously subsidized by the Servicemen's Readjustment Act of 1944, more popularly called the "GI Bill," ex-servicemen were more interested in pursuing a practical education that would equip them for good jobs in the booming postwar economy than in studying the liberal arts exclusively. Of the eleven million veterans of World War II, fully one-third decided to enter colleges and universities with full financial support from the federal government. Before the GI Bill, 6 percent of the population had graduated from college; the figure now rose dramatically to 20 percent. Never before or after would Saint Mary's have such a built-in clientele, and no one was going to look this gift horse in the mouth. Having earlier fully supported the wartime liberal arts program, Brother Austin was now willing to jettison important parts of it. Although he decided to retain the Great Books seminars, the president resurrected the three schools and traditional majors.

Chapter 10

The Korean War Crisis

·····························

The Presidency of Brother Thomas Levi, 1950–1956

On June 25, 1950, the massed armies of Communist North Korea lunged across the thirty-eighth parallel into the Republic of South Korea. Two days later, President Harry S Truman deployed American naval and air forces to bolster the rapidly retreating South Korean army. Draft calls were increased, and over the summer, college students across the country wondered if they would be returning to school in the fall or preparing for combat in Korea. The Christian Brothers at Saint Mary's College had worries of their own. The school was still carrying a heavy mortgage and could ill afford another sudden drop in enrollment. It had survived the Great Depression and the Second World War by a combination of luck, grit, outside help and government payments, but another national emergency coming in rapid succession might just push it over the brink. Things got very grim when enrollment in the fall of 1970 dropped from approximately 600 to 400 and then to 250 in the spring.

A month after the outbreak of the Korean War, as Saint Mary's was about to enter one of its most perilous periods, Brother Austin's third term as president expired. He had hoped the visitor would renew it, but Brother Alfred was upset by his outbursts and his cavalier attitude toward higher superiors. As a result, Brother Thomas Levi, the acting novice master, was named the new president. Although his family name sounds Jewish, Brother Thomas was in fact a florid Irishman. Unlike his predecessor, he lacked

Brother Thomas Levi, president during the Korean War Crisis. *Courtesy of the Christian Brothers Archives, Napa.*

a graduate degree; fortunately, he had been able to cobble together a BA only five years before becoming president. Honestly acknowledging his deficiencies both in academic credentials and collegiate experience, Brother Thomas later claimed that he told the provincial when informed of his appointment, "I can't believe that you would do a thing like this!"[195]

DROPPING FOOTBALL

When Brother Thomas first arrived on campus, Brother Austin pulled him aside to tender some important personal advice. "Thomas," he said, "you are going to find out, and I hope sooner than later, that you are either going to be a director, or a president. You can't be both. What they need right now is a president." This turned about to be sound advice. In other respects, Brother Austin was less helpful in prepping Brother Thomas for his new position. When Brother Austin caught his successor reviewing the college's financial records, he snatched them from his hands and warned, "Don't waste your time with those, and don't let anyone else get to them either."[196]

To keep the peace, Brother Thomas did not press the issue. However, once Brother Austin left campus in August, he got hold of these crucial spreadsheets, ran his eyes up and down their columns and then nearly suffered a nervous breakdown. *The College would be unable to meet its upcoming payroll!* Over the past three years, big-time football had drained the school dry. Brother Alfred Brousseau, now the provincial, immediately secured a bank loan of $50,000 to keep the doors open. However, when Brother Thomas asked for additional assistance a few months later, Brother Alfred

A pregame bonfire in the heyday of Saint Mary's football. *Courtesy of the Saint Mary's College Archives, Moraga.*

set down strict conditions, which the college's community council rejected. Caught between the proverbial rock and the hard place, Brother Thomas offered, in effect, to resign in November, only months after taking office.[197]

After he was refused, the new president decided that he had no alternative but to cut the faculty in half and to drop intercollegiate football. Archbishop Mitty concurred at a special meeting. During the 1950 season, Saint Mary's lost a staggering $125,000. The final game against Villanova drew only 150 fans to rain-soaked Kezar Stadium. Gross receipts amounted to a measly $658, but Villanova's guarantee was $15,000. During the entire season, the Galloping Gaels had won only two games. The high point was a 7–7 tie against Georgia in Kezar Stadium; the game marked the first time this Deep South team had ever competed against an African American player—in this instance, the versatile John Henry Johnson, who later went on to play for several professional teams, including the San Francisco 49ers.[198]

Within days of the announcement that football was being dropped, rumors began flying around the Bay Area that the college itself was about to go under. On January 7, 1951, the *San Francisco Examiner* reported on its front

John Henry Johnson, the first African American to play against Georgia. *Courtesy of the Saint Mary's College Archives, Moraga.*

page that Brother Thomas was on his way to Washington to seek federal aid. Although he succeeded in establishing the Western Training Center for the Federal Civil Defense Administration on campus, it remained for only two years and brought in only $36,000 in annual rent. As fiscal problems worsened, the provincial kept sending suggestions on how to dig out of the hole into which the college fallen. He urged the president to appeal to the alumni, create a scholarship fund to attract more students, offer more "bread and butter" courses and resurrect the high school department. Even while working to save Saint Mary's, Brother Alfred seriously proposed on two separate occasions the option of closing it either partially or completely.[199] He also floated the idea of acquiring "a more modest" location in a large metropolitan area such as Los Angeles or moving the school to a more populous city bordering San Francisco Bay.[200] This was not the first time district officials had concluded that building Saint Mary's in the "sticks" had been a huge mistake. Earlier, Brother Jasper Fitzsimmons, the visitor during the Second World War, had suggested selling Saint Mary's to the navy and establishing a day school in Oakland.[201]

The Christian Brothers Province Comes to the Rescue

Before his term ended in 1959, Brother Alfred would be compelled to give Saint Mary's College more than $1 million in assistance. This was a large sum of money, but the district easily had the means to give it. By the mid-'50s, Brother Alfred had settled accounts with the motherhouse in Rome for back taxes, and the province had accumulated more than $640,000 in a trust fund set up by his predecessor for future emergencies.[202] In a financial report that Brother Alfred issued in March 1955, he figured it would cost the district around $300,000 each year to support Saint Mary's College, pay for the education of the student brothers and cover its administrative costs.[203] Although he implied that this was a staggering sum for the province to cover, it really wasn't. Annual profits of the brothers' wineries in Napa and Reedley in the 1950s were more than adequate to meet all these expenses with money to spare. In the fiscal year of 1949, ending on March 31, the district's net income after novitiate expenses was $798,961 with no taxes being paid; in 1950, it was $1,068,543 with no taxes being paid; in 1951, it was $2,224,684 with no taxes being paid; in 1952, it was $260,870 after taxes were either being paid or sequestered; in 1954, it was $629,194 (adjusted to $576,593 following an audit) after tax provision had been made and novitiate and school expenses deducted; and in 1955, it was $613,829 (adjusted to $587,555 following an audit) again after tax provision had been made and novitiate and school expenses had been deducted.[204] No records are available in the archives for the year 1953. In short, provincial annual income far outpaced expenses throughout Brother Thomas's term as president. Early in 1955, Brother Alfred even decided one day, perhaps on an impulse, to pay off what remained of the mortgage owed to Archbishop Mitty.[205] At last, the brothers had gotten back the deed to their school.

Brother Thomas was well aware that the financially strapped college could not continue to rely on Mont La Salle Vineyards for assistance but needed to develop new sources of revenue. To this end, he established a thirty-two-person Board of Regents in 1952. It is not to be confused with the Board of Trustees, which actually governs the institution. The regents are men and women, often from the world of business and finance, who advise school officials on fundraising matters. Later, they would help manage its modest endowment portfolio. Although Brother Alfred wanted Saint Mary's to become "self-sufficient," he had his doubts about the Board of Regents because he didn't want the brothers "consorting with the wealthy." This was not something they normally did, and the founder had frowned upon it.[206] Brother Thomas thought otherwise. He purchased a box at the San Francisco opera house to increase visibility, visited the homes of affluent San Franciscans and dined at San Francisco's finest restaurants, especially at Jack's, his absolute favorite. Once in a society page picture, he was mistakenly identified as the son of James David Zellerbach of the Crown Zellerbach Corporation. Brother Thomas thought it was a "scream,"[207] but Brother Alfred was not happy.

The Integrated Liberal Arts Program

At the same time Saint Mary's was fighting to keep its doors open, it was struggling to preserve its academic integrity. In the spring of 1953, a team from the Western Association of Schools and Colleges visited campus and expressed grave concerns about the school's shaky finances, low enrollment and academic health. The campus visitors were so worried by what they had found that the accrediting agency granted Saint Mary's College accreditation for only two years.[208] Something had to be done to strengthen the school academically.

Through the assistance of graduates and friends of the college, Brother Thomas was able to secure a grant from the Rosenberg Foundation in 1955 to underwrite a two-year "experimental" program in the liberal arts. With this funding, Professor Hagerty, working with the Institute for Philosophical Studies in San Francisco, was able to set up what came to be known as the "Integrated Liberal Arts Curriculum" in the following year. It bore a strong resemblance to the wartime Great Books Program that Brother Austin had largely dismantled in 1945, although this latest version grouped texts around large themes such as "Man," "Nature" and "God" and enrolled only a select group of students. In effect, the Integrated Program became a college within the college. After a year in operation, it was criticized by three consulting professors for relying too heavily on short extracts from a variety of works. They recommended that in the future a few longer works of central importance be read, but still around one of the "Great Themes." However, when Brother Robert Smith became the program director a year later, when Hagerty became gravely ill, the new liberal arts program began to follow the Saint John's model; this meant that the thematic approach gave way to the chronological reading of the Great Books within large historical epochs.

In the late summer of 1957, the founder of the Integrated Program, Dr. Hagerty, died of leukemia at the young age of fifty-eight, with Brother Thomas at his bedside. In a tribute read into the *Congressional Record* of the Eighty-fifth Congress by his former student, Congressman George P. Miller, Hagerty's rich contributions to his alma mater were lovingly detailed, including his sponsorship of the curricular revolution in 1942, his co-editorship of the *Moraga Quarterly* and his constant championing of the Great Books and the seminar method of teaching. At the funeral Mass, former student Father Stanley Parmisano, OP, declared in his eulogy of Hagerty: "He believed in the workings of the human mind and its capacity to reach the truth of things…[He wanted] to hear what his students found in a given book or life situation rather than tell them what he himself found there; wanting them to grow from within rather than be stretched and hammered into misshape from without."[209]

THE CHRISTIAN BROTHERS AND THE LIBERAL ARTS

Four years before the implementation of the Rosenberg Grant, the Christian Brothers in the United States, including those at Saint Mary's College, celebrated in the spring of 1951 the three-hundred-year anniversary of the birth of Saint John Baptist De La Salle. The most significant commemorative event took place at Saint Mary's College's sister institution, Manhattan College in the Bronx. On April 30, 1951, the French philosopher Jacques Maritain gave what must be regarded as one of the most important addresses in the history of the Brothers of the Christian Schools. After praising the American brothers for entering secondary and collegiate education and teaching the classics, he asked an important rhetorical question: "Do you think that St. Jean-Baptiste de la Salle would have been astonished at the unforeseen developments taken by his schools in America?" Maritain's answer was an emphatic "no." The founder, he insisted, would have "rejoiced" over and "approved" of the "change" made by the American brothers because they were merely altering the "means" and not the ultimate goals he had had in mind.[210]

In his letter to the General Chapter in 1923, Cardinal Gasparri, Maritain recalled, had stated that "the teaching of the classics" should not alter the basic nature of the institute whose "principal end" was, had been and ought always to remain "the school for poor." But how was it possible,

Maritain wondered, for His Eminence to bring together in a single sentence the phrases "teaching of the classics" and "the school of the poor?" This seemed, on the face of it, a contradiction in terms. But not to Maritain. From "the point of view of the history of culture," he argued, all human beings are by their nature intellectually impoverished, no matter the social class to which they might accidentally belong. "For we are poor rational animals, and as Aristotle put it," he went on to say, "the highest achievements of knowledge are but precarious possessions for us." Only through the liberal arts could anyone hope to find true "liberation of mind." "We might also submit," Maintain went on to say, "that if the 'teaching of the classics' and the 'school for the poor' are to be brought together, this means finally that the cultural and intellectual heritage of mankind has to be made available, as American education seeks to do, for young people from all walks of life. In this perspective the particular occurrence I am now discussing, the task assumed by the Christian Brothers in liberal education, under the incentive of the American bishops, appears as a token of that liberal education for all which is to be expected, I believe, from the future of our civilization."[211] In adopting the Integral Liberal Arts Program, as it later came to be called, and continuing to offer Great Books seminars to all students, Saint Mary's College during the Korean War period was fulfilling this clarion call to provide a liberal arts education to young men of all social classes, from the poor to the very rich.

Combating the Cult of Ignorance

At the same time more California brothers were earning advanced degrees and Saint Mary's College was strengthening its liberal arts curriculum, Brother Alfred was forced to wage a concerted campaign against what he courageously and accurately called a "cult of ignorance"[212] in the institute, emanating from higher superiors in Europe. Sometime in 1957, he received a set of "General Directives" from the newly elected superior general, Brother Nicet-Joseph Loubet, warning him of the dangers of permitting Christian Brothers to pursue advanced studies in institutions of higher learning. "Higher profane studies," Brother Nicet-Joseph declared, using all capital letters to underscore his point, "are not necessarily a good thing—either for the individual brother or for the institute as a whole." Permitting brothers to study at universities was inherently dangerous because it brought them into close contact with the "world," with "ideas" confusing to "faith" and with members of the opposite sex. Moreover, brothers with advanced degrees were often "difficult to manage," "less devoted" and more "egocentric" than their less privileged and less well-educated confreres. In the superior general's directives, one catches echoes of the old fear of producing too many "patricians" in an order that should be composed mainly of lowly "plebeians." The superior general therefore urged local superiors to carefully screen potential candidates for advanced studies and, more importantly, not to take on too many institutions that required doctoral degrees. "We were founded first and foremost for the artisans and the poor…for those belonging to what is known as the working class," he reiterated, in the language of his predecessors. "We can never do too much to efficiently carry out this type of work." It was important to train capable teachers, Brother Nicet-Joseph was willing to concede, but only in a manner that did not expose them to the "many dangers…met with in higher studies." "AS A RESULT," he concluded, resorting once again to the upper case, as if to shout, "WE SHOULD BE EXTREMELY CAREFUL ON THIS POINT."[213]

The superior general's letter may have been applicable to other regions of the institute, where Christian Brothers taught primarily in grammar schools, orphanages and technical institutes. However, it betrayed an ignorance of the unique educational system that the Christian Brothers had established in the United States as far back as the late nineteenth century. The French superiors general seemed incapable of grasping the concept of class mobility through a liberal arts education. Brother Nicet-Joseph's directives clearly demonstrate that the essential issues at the heart of the Latin Question were alive and kicking as late as the 1950s. They would not be finally laid to rest until the following decade, when the first non-Frenchman was elected superior general in 1966 at the time of Vatican II. He was an American with a PhD in Latin from the Catholic University of America.

Chapter 11
Changing Times

·······························

*The Presidencies of Brother Albert Plotz and
Brother Michael Quinn, 1956–1969*

I n 1956, when Brother Thomas's second term expired, prominent regents
and trustees decided to lobby for his retention or at least for making
him the director of development
to keep Saint Mary's on the
"upswing." They made their case
to the provincial, but he had
already decided to remove Brother
Thomas because of his growing
"popularity" with the wealthy elite
of San Francisco.[214] In place of
Brother Thomas, Brother Alfred
appointed his mirror opposite.
The new president, Brother
Albert Plotz, was a model of
religious regularity and punctilious
efficiency. Respectful of superiors,
he would make no major decisions
without first consulting the visitor.
In contrast to the smooth and
sociable Brother Thomas, Brother
Albert was a very private person
who seldom showed any emotion.

Brother Albert Plotz, president during
the 1950s. *Courtesy of the Christian Brothers
Archives, Napa.*

He was not the "glad hand" type, as Brother Thomas had surely been.[215] Although Brother Albert did not hold an advanced degree, he demonstrated, as he thought any good college president should, "genuine interest in scholarship" and "respect for scholars."[216] Neither the gregarious promoter nor the accomplished academician, he was a reliable company man.

EXPANDING AND DEVELOPING THE COLLEGE

During his years as president, Brother Albert worked hard to enlarge the student body. On March 9, 1958, he presided over an "Open House Day" to familiarize prospective students and their parents with the beautiful Moraga campus. He also appointed John W. Scudder the school's first lay director of admissions. Within a year, Scudder increased the size of the school from 781 to 850 students. The goal was to reach 1,000 in the near future, which is somewhat less than what Archbishop Alemany had had in mind when he founded Saint Mary's back in 1863.

In his efforts to raise more revenue, Brother Albert established the college's first Development Office in 1957. It received enthusiastic support from a visitor tired of pouring money into the college. However, Brother Alfred was worried about the temptations that might beset the first vice-president for development, Brother Xavier Joy, as he courted potential donors and benefactors. He therefore forbade him to visit the homes of potential donors because a brother might become "quite friendly and intimate, not only with the men but also with the women of the household."[217]

Building on Brother Thomas's contacts, Brother Albert sought to attract new friends and contributors to the college, especially from the business community. In 1957, Saint Mary's sponsored its first annual "Executive Symposium," a two-day overnight conference that drew local business leaders to the campus for talks, panel discussions and seminars on a wide variety of economic issues. Governor Ronald Reagan was the featured speaker at one of these events.

In his last years in office, Brother Albert began to give serious thought to upgrading the campus. Writing to Archbishop Mitty early in 1959, he noted that because of "our expanding enrollment, this program would include the construction of two residence halls, enlargement of the gymnasium, a student union, a fine arts building and a new library." The costs of this expansion were estimated at over $2 million, with $900,000

Brother Michael Quinn and Governor Ronald Reagan at an Executive Symposium.
Courtesy of the Christian Brothers Archives, Napa.

of it coming from long-term government loans and the remainder from a fundraising campaign.[218]

In the fall of 1960, a fifty-two-room dormitory was built perpendicular to nearby Aquinas Hall. It was fitting that the first building erected since 1928 was named for Mitty. In the following year, Saint Mary's added another residence hall to the campus and named it in honor of Brother

Justin. Financing for the new buildings came mainly from low-interest loans provided by the United States Housing and Home Financing Agency, marking the beginning of an increasingly close relationship between governmental agencies and the college, not only in terms of providing funds for construction but also for scholarships and grants for potential students.

As president, Brother Albert did not make any major changes in the undergraduate curriculum, which a WASC visitation fortunately judged to be in good shape. A report issued late in 1959 declared that "the team was impressed by the general buoyancy of the College and the confident expectation of continued improvement."[219] In 1958, Saint Mary's established two new graduate summer school programs. For lack of students, the philosophy program folded four years later. The new master's in contemporary theology not only survived but also prospered over the next twenty-five years. As a result of the dramatic decline of sisters and brothers in the United States after Vatican II, enrollment in the program dropped off, and it was phased out in the early 1980s, although the last degree was granted in 1987.

STUDENT LIFE IN THE '50s

During Brother Albert's presidency, Saint Mary's students engaged in what later became a world-famous campus caper. In late 1958, attempting to

World-famous photo of the phone booth stuffing in 1959. *With the permission of Joe Munroe.*

beat a record set in Durban, South Africa, the residents of Aquinas Hall packed into the downstairs telephone closet but found it was too small for their purposes. Later, a Plexiglas Pacific Telephone & Telegraph booth was set up on the lawn in front of the chapel. Then, in a crosshatch pattern, twenty-three (or twenty-two) students packed themselves in, layer-by-layer, with extremities poking out. In March 1959, *Life* magazine published a full-page picture of the phone booth stuffing, and it has since become an icon of the Eisenhower era.

The 1950s marked a revival of religion in the United States. At Saint Mary's, the most active student clubs on campus were the Knights of Columbus and the Legion of Mary. The apostolic work of the latter group "included the maintenance of a religious bulletin board, circulation of Legion of Decency lists [of approved movies], the teaching of catechism and active campaigning to increase attendance at nightly prayers and rosary in the chapel." Saint Mary's students were periodically required to attend Mass, usually on First Fridays; make annual student retreats; and participate in assemblies on Catholic religious topics. Later in the decade, a vocal minority began to question administrative paternalism, most especially prior censorship of the school newspapers. In the fall of 1961, John Miles, the *Collegian* editor, resigned over this issue, illicitly published his own letter of resignation and was suspended from school by Brother Albert. The president's draconian action was not the least bit exceptional. A University of San Francisco student commented at the time, "Editorial shakeups were as common in the Bay Area [Catholic colleges and universities] last week as sunbathers in the Park."[220]

BROTHER MICHAEL QUINN BECOMES PRESIDENT

On January 29, 1962, a car carrying a group of Christian Brothers back to Saint Mary's College from the Heavenly Valley ski resort near Lake Tahoe skidded off an icy curve on Highway 50 east of Placerville, rolled down a twenty-foot embankment and then crashed against some large boulders a few feet from the cascading American River. Two passengers in the backseat escaped with minor injuries, but three other brothers were killed almost instantly when they were thrown from the car and crushed to death.[221] Dead were the driver, Brother Albert Plotz, the president of Saint Mary's; Brother Cornelius Braeg; and Brother Julius Rodriquez-Paneda, a retired professor

Brother Michael Quinn, president during the centennial year. *Courtesy of Christian Brothers Archives, Napa.*

of romance languages. News of the terrible accident sent shock waves throughout the San Francisco District and the Saint Mary's College community. A solemn requiem Mass was celebrated for the three brothers at old Saint Mary's Cathedral on Van Ness Street in San Francisco, with high government and ecclesiastical officials in attendance.

A few days after the car accident that claimed Brother Albert's life, a new provincial, Brother Jerome West, named Brother Michael Quinn the twenty-third president of Saint Mary's College. A psychology professor, Brother Michael became only the second president to hold an earned doctorate. He had studied for his degree in clinical psychology at Loyola University of Chicago, specializing in the interpretation of the Thematic Apperception Test. A lifelong fan of the movies of Alfred Hitchcock, Brother Michael himself bore a passing physical resemblance to the jowly director and, like him, could also be droll, witty and enigmatic.[222]

At the time of Brother Michael's appointment, the visitor decided at long last to separate the academic and religious duties of the president of the college. Henceforth, the president would function only as the chief administrator of the institution; another brother would be appointed to serve as the canonical superior of the religious community on campus. In a news release, Brother Jerome explained his reasons for the change: "The rapid academic advances and the increased enrollment under Brother Albert's administration has increased the administrative burdens of the president. With the approach of the College Centennial in 1963 and a major building program now in the planning stage, the office of President has been separated from that of superior of the religious community."[223]

Not long after taking office, Brother Michael decided to create the new office of academic vice-president and to conduct a national search for a

Dr. Rafael Alan Pollock, first lay academic vice-president. *Courtesy of the Saint Mary's College Archives, Moraga.*

qualified Catholic layman to fill it. This was a major moment in the history of Saint Mary's College, marking the first in a series of critical appointments that would place more and more of the key offices on campus in the hands of lay persons rather than in those of the Christian Brothers. Brother Michael finally settled on Rafael Alan Pollock, a young, bespectacled Yale PhD who was then teaching English literature at Notre Dame University. A family man with several children and a convert to Catholicism, Pollock assumed his new post at Saint Mary's College in the fall of 1962.

The Centennial Year and Century II Campaign

On taking office, Brother Michael's chief concern was preparing for the yearlong celebration of the college's centennial. The festivities commenced in the fall of 1962 and concluded in the spring of 1963. The year got underway in fine fashion on October 4, 1962, when two thousand visitors converged on Moraga for Brother Michael's colorful inauguration. The featured speaker was Vice President Lyndon Baines Johnson, who arrived in spectacular style aboard a helicopter. Congratulating Saint Mary's College for centering its centennial on the theme of "the liberal arts as the language of free men," Johnson said that he sometimes feared "that in this age of technology we seem to forget that machines were made for Man and not Man for machines."[224] In his own remarks, Brother Michael asserted that Saint Mary's could no longer afford to be a Catholic "ghetto." The time had come to communicate with the "rest of the human race," even with nonbelievers.[225]

Brother Michael Quinn bestowing an honorary degree on Vice President Lyndon B. Johnson. *Courtesy of Saint Mary's College Archives, Moraga.*

In association with the centennial celebrations, Saint Mary's launched an ambitious ten-year fundraising and development campaign dubbed Century II. Its goal was to raise $11 million, of which less than $2 million was earmarked for buildings and renovation projects. The bulk of the funds would be used for such things as increased faculty salaries and library improvements. The strong academic emphasis of the Century II campaign can be glimpsed in a remarkable statement issued by the Development

Office: "Saint Mary's College does not intend to engage in a contest for size of enrollment or physical plant, but has as its goal to provide the academic programs and facilities through which the students may obtain the best possible liberal arts education."[226] In 1969, Brother Xavier, the driving force behind the centennial celebrations and Century II campaign, withdrew from the institute to marry one of the wealthy matrons he had ostensibly been courting for the college, unfortunately confirming Brother Alfred's worst fears about the dangers of consorting with lay donors and their wives.

Although most of the Century II campaign funds were devoted to academic enrichment, some were set aside for building projects, including the construction of a badly needed new library. Although work on the structure began in 1965, it took more than two years to complete because

Saint Albert Hall, built in 1967. *Courtesy of Saint Mary's College Archives, Moraga.*

of unexpected soil problems. Funding was provided by almost $1 million in federal grants and low-interest government loans and by a gift of $200,000 from Clay Bedford, a Saint Mary's Regent, as well as by donations from various alumni and friends of the school. The new library, named Saint Albert Hall in honor of the great Dominican theologian and in memory of the late Brother Albert Plotz, was blessed and dedicated on April 28, 1967, as part of a weekend celebration that included a seminar on American life, Alumni Homecoming and a campus open house. Even some of the structure's earlier detractors found it quite beautiful when unveiled. It was unfortunate that it did not incorporate overhanging roofs, as the other buildings on campus did. Still, its whitewashed walls and slanted red tile roof helped to harmonize it with surrounding structures. The interior was open and lightsome.

The Revival of Football

As soon as Dr. Pollock arrived on campus, he sought to alter the college's longtime public image. He wanted people to regard Saint Mary's not as a former football factory but as a distinguished small liberal arts college. On May 12, 1963, the *San Francisco Examiner* published an article with this evocative headline: "New Image for St. Mary's: Instead of Galloping Gaels, Studious Air Prevails at 'Happy School's' Centennial."

However, three years later, a group of students succeeded in reviving football. After "Slip" Madigan died in October 1966, his ghost continued to haunt the campus. Gregory Aloia, a former high school football player who had been camping out in the equipment room of the campus gymnasium, later claimed that one night Slip appeared to him in a dream and personally commissioned him to bring football back to Saint Mary's. Fired by this improbable, although apparently vivid, experience, Aloia was able to enlist a significant number of recruits in a crusade to revive intercollegiate football as a "club" sport, despite the opposition of the president and the bulk of the faculty. The resurrected team got off to a flying start in the fall of 1967 and went undefeated, but against weak competition. The official program for the Saint Mary's–University of San Francisco game on October 20, 1967, invoked the "legend of the '30s" with this exuberant exclamation: "Spirited by the records and memories of Slip Madigan's giant killers, students made football more than a memory, more than a dream—it was a reality."

In the same year football returned to Saint Mary's College, the mood on campus changed dramatically. The era of the "Old Gaels," only recently revived, quickly faded into the background. Now grape boycotts and civil rights became heated topics of conversation on campus; probably the most divisive question under debate was whether the United States should withdraw unilaterally from the increasingly unpopular war in Vietnam. California state senator George Miller Jr., in his address at the dedication of the new library, had rhetorically asked his audience through an interlocutor whether we must "fight on in Vietnam solely because we are there?"[227] For many Americans, especially male college students subject to the draft, the answer was a resounding "no."

During the late '60s, Saint Mary's students organized "teach-ins" against the Vietnam War, held draft card burnings outside the new library, demanded that Hi Continental Food Services stop serving grapes not picked by the United Farm Workers, expressed sympathy for and solidarity with those Berkeley students who had been arrested for occupying Sproul Hall, gave folk singer Joan Baez a standing ovation when she appeared on campus to speak on the power of nonviolent protest and listened in rapt attention in the little theater to Bobby Seale as he defended the tactics of the Black Panthers and condemned the racism and brutality of the Oakland Police Department. In the spring of 1965, Brother Michael secretly flew to Alabama to join Martin Luther King in the Selma March for voting rights. No one on campus knew of his whereabouts for several days, not even his own secretary. His attendance at the Edmund Pettis Bridge with Dr. King would prove a life-changing experience. When he returned, he was determined to do more to attract minority students to Saint Mary's.[228]

STUDENTS FOR PROGRESSIVE ACTION NOW (SPAN)

Throughout the 1960s, college students in the United States demanded a more "relevant" education linked to the great social issues of the day. The first demands at Saint Mary's for curricular change were voiced in the spring of 1968, when a group of students campaigned for a reduction in the number of philosophy course requirements. At the time, liberal arts students were required to take seventeen units of philosophy for graduation; this may well have been the highest such requirement of any college or university in the United States. It wasn't just the sheer number of units that rankled many

Saint Mary's students but what they regarded as the closed-mindedness of professors in the Philosophy Department. Largely through a petition drive, activists were able to persuade the faculty to reduce upper-division philosophy requirements from nine to six units of a student's choice.

This reform turned out to be a dress rehearsal for more radical revisions that would take place during the next academic year. Acceding to student activists, Dr. Pollock announced that on October 29, 1968—officially called a "Day of Inquiry" but popularly known as "Sanguine Tuesday"—all classes would be cancelled so that professors and students could gather in Madigan Gymnasium to discuss the meaning of the liberal arts at Saint Mary's, its Catholic character and various proposals for curricular changes that had been floating around campus. The number of students who attended the general "bitch-in," faculty-student luncheon and departmental meetings was disappointing. Undaunted by the apathy of the passive majority, a group of about one hundred students, led by student body president Daniel Whitehurst, met in February 1969, formed themselves into SPAN and began pushing for a broad range of curricular and calendar reforms. In an article published in the *Collegian* on April 2, Dennis Flanagan traced the genesis of SPAN back to larger developments, events and protests in this country and in Europe:

> *back to the Free Speech Movement in Berkeley, back to the anguish over the growing involvement in Vietnam and the formation of the Viet Nam Day Committee; and back to the riots in Watts and elsewhere. Its seeds were planted in the snows of New Hampshire, by the gymnasium at Columbia University, along the barricades of May in France, and in the streets of Chicago. In all those places and more the spirit of questioning and [the] desire for change here originated.* [229]

In February 1969, shortly after SPAN came into being, student leaders presented Dr. Pollock with a list of twenty-seven proposed reforms under the banner of the "Moraga Manifesto." This comprehensive platform called, among other things, for the adoption of the 4-1-4 school calendar pioneered by Florida Presbyterian College; the abolition of all required courses; the introduction of coeducation in the next academic year; and the recruitment of more minority students, more non-Catholics and more non-Californians. [230] During a thirty-day period in the spring semester of 1969, the faculty voted favorably on one SPAN proposal after another, effecting in a relatively short time an educational revolution at Saint Mary's. The old system of numerous breadth requirements in philosophy, theology, history, government, foreign language, science and mathematics was discarded, along with the Great Books Seminars introduced during World War II. Eight so-called Collegiate Seminars were instituted to replace both of them. In five of these core courses, professors and students would read together and discuss both classical and contemporary texts around a great theme such as "The Nature of Self," "The Nature of Mind," "The Nature of Society" and "The Nature of Nature." Some of the books to be read in these new required seminars would be prescribed; others would be selected by the individual professor, who would be required to provide a rationale for his inclusion. A Collegiate Seminar Governing Committee, appointed by the academic vice-president, would supervise the new core program, which aimed not to cover subject matter but rather to develop the minds and hearts of the students. Two of the eight Collegiate Seminars, placed under the control of the Religious Studies Department, would be devoted to raising fundamental questions about man's quest for ultimate meaning and his response to Christian revelation. Another, under the aegis of the Political Science Department, would concentrate on key texts of American political philosophy, under the title of "Man and Government." The old system of two long semesters was discarded; students would now take four courses of equal value in the spring and fall terms and one course during the January intersession when they would be able to travel abroad and pursue independent study projects.

Whitehurst Returns to Campus

Ten years after the SPAN revolution, the mood in Moraga had dramatically changed. The Vietnam War was over, the farm labor controversy had been settled and protest marches had petered out. Students seemed uninterested in political and social questions. Many were content to drink beer in their dormitory rooms and toss Frisbees on the lawn outside De La Salle Hall. They worried about the "real world" only as graduation approached. It was as if, in some important respects, the '50s had returned to campus. The musical *Grease*, a pleasant, tuneful spoof of the decade, was a big hit on campus in the spring.

As if the muses of history were directing events, the senior class of 1978 decided to invite Daniel Whitehurst, the former SPAN leader and now the youngest mayor in Fresno's history, to deliver the major address at commencement ceremonies, mainly as the result of an article that the *Saint Mary's Collegian* had recently run on "campus politics" ten years earlier. Students were surprised to learn that Saint Mary's had produced its own "Mario Savio" in the late '60s and that SPAN had been able to make so many radical changes on campus in such a short time.[231] Old-time professors and current students looked forward to what Whitehurst might say in his speech. Fears that he would relight the fires of protest proved groundless. Dressed in a dark business suit, he spoke to the graduates in a quiet, almost offhanded manner. It was time, he said in Kennedyesque terms, that people asked what they could do for society rather than what society could do for them. Whitehurst did not speak all that much about the SPAN days, except to say that the movement had grown out of a genuine love for Saint Mary's College and a deep desire to make it a better place in which to learn and live.

Whether the SPAN movement had made Saint Mary's a better place in which to learn and live is the key question, of course. Many professors who supported the movement would probably answer that it did. They would argue that today the college is more open, more free and more pluralistic. It has outgrown its immigrant origins and can no longer be fairly described as a refuge for Irish and Italian male Catholics on the rise. Others who lived through the SPAN years may want to emphasize what has been lost. Before the '60s, a certain masculine mystique and traditional religious spirit pervaded the campus and gave many of its all-male students a strong sense of being part of a unique place and unique experience. Where else were the classical tradition, the Great Books and the Catholic faith taken so seriously? Where else would a campus club be named, mockingly, for Plotinus? Personal biases aside, it may finally be impossible to determine objectively whether SPAN destroyed the myth of "a little white academic city" of classicism and traditional Catholicism or simply opened Saint Mary's College at long last to a wider world of people and ideas. In a similar vein, the continuing historical debates over the positive and negative consequences of the '60s social movements continue to divide Americans.

Chapter 12

Years of Turmoil,
Years of Progress

· ·

The Presidency of Brother Mel Anderson,
1969–1997

After two terms in office, Brother Michael Quinn was tired and wanted out. Partly on his recommendation, a new provincial, Brother Bertram Coleman, selected forty-year-old Brother Mel Anderson as the college's twenty-third president. A redheaded, lanky man of Irish and Swedish descent, he had earned his bachelor's degree at Saint Mary's in 1952. Most of his educational career in the Christian Brothers had been spent teaching at or serving as the vice-principal or principal of high schools in Napa, San Francisco, Pasadena, Fresno and Berkeley. A campus report in 1977 would question whether extensive experience in secondary school administration was the best training ground for a college president and whether it prepared a candidate to understand the complex workings of a collegiate

Brother Mel Anderson, president for twenty-eight years. *Courtesy of Christian Brothers Archives, Napa.*

academic community.[232] Brother Mel himself wondered about his academic and administrative preparation for the presidency when the visitor first offered him the post. Two weeks later, when he finally accepted, Brother Mel told Brother Bertram that he was free to consider his appointment merely "interim," which is ironic given that Brother Mel entered office on July 1, 1969, and did not leave until that same month and day in 1997.[233]

Building a New Saint Mary's

As a member of the Board of Trustees in the late '60s, Brother Mel was concerned that the campus, built back in 1928, had badly deteriorated over the years. As president, he was determined to refurbish, rebuild and renew Saint Mary's. Dedicated to the artistic vision of John J. Donovan, Brother Mel searched, upon taking office, for a campus architect who would respect and build on the Spanish Renaissance–California Mission design of the existing buildings. He quickly settled on Japanese American architect Kazuo Goto. A graduate of the UC School of Architecture, he had been sent to

Filippi Hall, built in 1991 in the Spanish Renaissance–California Mission style. *Courtesy of the Saint Mary's Archives, Moraga.*

Soda Activity Center, built in 1989 during Brother Mel's presidency. *Courtesy of the Saint Mary's Archives, Moraga.*

an internment camp during World War II. Brother Mel and Goto would forge a close working relationship based on the idea that developing the campus would be akin to building a cathedral in the Middle Ages—each succeeding addition would remain faithful to the original vision, producing over the years a satisfying organic whole.[234] It was intended that a visitor would have a hard time figuring out the date when buildings were erected because of their timeless beauty and basic uniformity. By the end of his twenty-eight years in office, Brother Mel had become the second builder of Saint Mary's, next to Brother Joseph Fenlon, as dormitories, classroom and administration buildings, student centers and athletic facilities mushroomed across the campus.

"HERE COME THE SKIRTS"

Early in his first term, Brother Mel decided the time had come to make Saint Mary's College a coeducational institution. Much groundwork had already been prepared. Admitting women had been one of SPAN's major proposals,

Becket Hall, built in 1968 to accommodate female students. *Courtesy of the Saint Mary's College Archives, Moraga.*

Women's NAIA Soccer Champions, 1984. *Courtesy of the Saint Mary's College Archives, Moraga.*

and Brother Michael had earlier decided to build two new dormitories, More and Becket Halls, in such a fashion that they could easily accommodate female students. Santa Clara University and the University of San Francisco had already gone "co-ed," leaving Saint Mary's, literally speaking, the "odd man out" among local, formerly all-male Catholic colleges. In his memoirs, Brother Mel says that he favored admitting women because "the chances for student body growth, subsequent academic enhancement and financial stability were unlikely" without going co-ed.[235]

SAVING FOOTBALL

As a high school principal, Brother Mel favored the performing arts over interscholastic athletics. In November 1957, he wrote an article for the *Religious Educator*, an in-house San Francisco District religion journal, praising La Salle High School in Pasadena, where he was then serving as its first vice-principal, for not fielding a football team when it opened a year earlier. However, when Brother Mel arrived at Saint Mary's, he changed his mind. He now judged that football would attract more students, help keep up minority enrollment, appeal to the alumni and keep Saint Mary's in the public eye.[236] Despite opposition from the bulk of the faculty and many students, the Board of Trustees decided in March 1970 not only to pay off the football club's debts but also to make football a college sport on the Division III or non-scholarship level and to fund the program from general revenues. In 1973, the college's first-ever football stadium was built at the rear of the campus at a cost of $250,000.

CAMPUS PROTESTS

Brother Mel had hardly settled into office when the campus faced student protests. The first threatened in March 1970 during an upcoming basketball game between Saint Mary's College and Brigham Young University, when several faculty members and students, upset that the Mormon Church denied the full priesthood to African Americans, were planning to mount a protest in the school gymnasium. A larger protest erupted in late April, after President Nixon widened the unpopular war in Vietnam by invading neighboring Cambodia. At Kent State University in Ohio, four students were shot and killed on May 4 by National Guard troops deployed to keep order. Campuses across the nation erupted. Student leaders at Saint Mary's called for a mass meeting in the campus quad to protest the shooting; 150 students showed up. A little later, the gathering grew to 300, and it was moved to Oliver Hall dining commons. There the students voted to go on strike. Saint Mary's became the second school in the nation to take such action, following the lead of Princeton. Hundreds of colleges and universities across the nation followed suit. On May 5, a plebiscite was held on campus to ratify the strike vote; the student body as a whole voted 450 to 19 in favor. On the same day, the faculty voted to shut down the school to the tumultuous ovation of 600 approving students. On May 6, 300 Saint Mary's students organized a bus and car caravan to Sacramento, where they met with six assembly members in a panel discussion on the war. The following day, students canvassed surrounding towns and dialogued with local residents about the war.

REPLACING DR. POLLOCK

After a trial year, Brother Mel concluded that Dr Pollock should be replaced as academic vice-president. Brother Mel disagreed with Pollock's views on academic standards, the recruitment of minority students and the school's Catholic character. In the spring of 1971, a search committee was appointed to find a suitable successor. It chose Dr. Thomas Slakey of St. John's College in Santa Fe. An alumnus, Slakey was a devout and articulate Roman Catholic, a faithful husband and devoted father to his four children and a reflective gentleman of the old school who smoked a pipe, wore conservative tweeds and favored quiet conversation. Much to Brother Mel's satisfaction, Dr. Slakey brought to Saint Mary's an abiding commitment to traditional liberal arts education and to the Catholic faith. In September 1971, the new AVP told the alumni magazine: "I am devoted to liberal arts colleges, and to Saint Mary's in particular…Indeed, I think that liberal education is of particular importance at this time, when the young seem less than ever disposed to be guided by established beliefs and customs and when they must genuinely make their own decisions of what is valuable in the past if they are to accept it at all."[237] In 1972, Slakey succeeded in restoring Great Books Seminars as electives, alongside of the theme-centered Collegiate Seminars initiated three years earlier.

The Odell Johnson Affair

Having placed academic affairs in the hands of a man he admired and trusted, Brother Mel turned his attention to improving what he regarded as unacceptable conditions in the residence halls. In the fall of 1971, he decided not to renew the contract of the dean of students, Odell Johnson. A soft-spoken African American, Johnson had been a star basketball player during his undergraduate years at Saint Mary's. Based on personal observations and consultations with the residence hall counselors over the previous two years, the president concluded that the dean was not working closely with the Christian Brothers and had failed to maintain a safe and studious atmosphere in the college's dormitories.[238] Nevertheless, support for the dean on campus was strong and widespread among both professors and students. Protest meetings were called, and petitions to retain Johnson were sent to the trustees with hundreds of signatures.

The discontent over the dean's dismissal spread into other areas of campus life, like ripples in a placid pond into which a stone had been tossed. A group of concerned white students came to Johnson's defense. Broadening

Dean Odell Johnson, whose release caused an uproar on campus. *Courtesy of the Saint Mary's College Archives, Moraga.*

their critique of Brother Mel's administration, they distributed flyers at the college's annual open house in January, questioning the institution's educational and building priorities. Just at the time Johnson's dismissal was causing an uproar on campus, racial tensions in the Athletic Department boiled over. Early in 1972, several black basketball players, upset with the "pro" coaching style of the basketball coach, presented a list of their grievances to the school's athletic director. Among other things, they wanted the Athletic Department to hire a black coach and establish some kind of grievance procedure. Convinced that their complaints were not being dealt with properly, they refused to suit up for a game with nearby Hayward State College. Later, in February, in the middle of a game with archrival Santa Clara, these same players walked off the court in support of Dean Johnson, yelling out to the startled crowd that racism was rampant on campus.

In an unfortunate instance of bad timing, on the Monday following the Santa Clara game, the college administration announced that several part-time minority professors would be released for financial reasons and several ethnic studies courses would be eliminated in the coming fall term because of low enrollments. This action further inflamed faculty members and students, who proceeded to vent their rage at an emotion-charged meeting held in the college gymnasium.

Up to this point, Chicano students had taken a backseat in campus protests. Now in March, they decided to move front and center. After a Sunday student Mass, they announced to startled worshipers that they intended to occupy the chapel and go on a water-only fast until their demands for better treatment had been met. A few brothers wanted to call in the local sheriff, and the bishop of Oakland threatened to excommunicate the protestors.

After several days of hard bargaining, Brother Mel signed an agreement with the protestors on March 19, 1972, accepting most, but not all, their demands for more minority instructors and more minority courses. However, he refused to rehire Dean Johnson or to exempt the striking basketball players from potential disciplinary action. In the spring of 1972, William McLeod, an alumnus who had been serving as the assistant superintendent of schools for the Fresno diocese, was named Johnson's successor.

Although Brother Mel does not admit to making major mistakes in his recently published memoirs, he comes very close in the case of Johnson's dismissal. He candidly concedes that "it might have been more prudential to renew the Dean's contract for an additional year, thus sending him the message that all was not well in his department and giving him, the administration and the faculty resident directors the time to reconsider, thus avoiding the confrontations which occurred at a difficult time in the history of both the College and the nation."[239] If Johnson had not been released, the open house demonstration, basketball walkout and chapel occupation might never have taken place, and the budget crisis, following on the bad publicity these incidents generated, might not have been so severe. A report commissioned by the Board of Trustees in the wake of the Odell Johnson Affair found deep divisions on campus but did not adequately acknowledge the impact on Saint Mary's of the turmoil convulsing the larger society.

When the fall term opened in 1972, the college faced a worsening financial crisis. Fears that the recent campus turmoil would drive away potential students had proved well founded. Enrollment dipped from an all-time high of 1,265 in the previous year to 1,029. By October, it had fallen to 950 students. At the end of the 1972–73 school year, the college's accrued deficit would climb to $766,000. Attempting to confront a serious financial crisis, Brother Mel was forced to take drastic measures. Non-academic personnel were released, departmental budgets were slashed and a hiring freeze was decreed.

In an attempt to keep the college deficit from ballooning, the Board of Trustees decided in the spring of 1974 to raise the student-faculty ratio to 13.5 to 1 and then, a little later, to 15 to 1. After finding his bearings, Dr. Slakey publicly objected to the higher figure because it would entail scheduling large lecture courses in order to offset small enrollments in majors such as foreign language, chemistry and mathematics. He pleaded with the trustees to gradually phase in the 15 to 1 ratio and rely more on increased enrollment to bridge the budget gap, but the board judged that the school's financial problems were so serious that it had no choice but to impose the higher ratio.

Brother Dominic Ruegg becomes Academic Vice-President

In August 1974, just before the fall term opened, Dr. Slakey suddenly resigned. A press release made it appear as if he had simply decided not to renew his contract. Such was not the case. The immediate cause of Dr. Slakey's resignation was Brother Mel's refusal to fire minority dean Thomas Brown, who had circulated a letter on campus critical of the AVP. However, this latest incident was probably just the last straw for Slakey. Not in the best of health, he had grown weary of having to carry bad news to the faculty. Modest and humble, a quiet scholar at heart, Slakey had little taste for constant confrontation. After teaching World Classics seminars for two years at Saint Mary's, this gentle and thoughtful man happily returned to Saint John's College in Santa Fe, where a place had been held open for him.

Faced with Dr. Slakey's sudden resignation, Brother Mel was forced to find a new academic vice-president on the fly. He quickly settled on Brother Dominic Ruegg, a classics professor, who was then engaged in underwater archaeological research off the coast of Mallorca, Spain. A gifted teacher, former academic dean and recent chairman of the faculty, he was urbane and erudite, with a doctorate from the Catholic University in Latin. Brother Dominic consented to serve as academic vice-president but with the understanding that he would seek to achieve financial stability for the college by adding new revenue-producing programs to the traditional undergraduate curriculum. This strategy appealed to Brother Mel, even though he had recruited Dr. Slakey precisely for his devotion to the traditional liberal arts. When Brother Dominic pushed through these new educational programs, sometimes bypassing the faculty, and increased the teaching load, morale on campus turned sour. For his part, he doubtless felt he was only saving the school from itself.

THE WASC VISIT OF 1975 AND ITS AFTERMATH

In November 1975, a WASC accreditation team arrived on campus for a periodic visit. From the administration's point of view, the visit could not have come at a worse moment. Brother Dominic was still settling into office, the financial crisis was deepening and morale on campus was as bad as it had ever been. Not surprisingly, the team found a crisis in communication on campus so severe as to imperil the institution's very survival. The final report reads: "The depth of concern we encountered for the future of the College is, tragically, matched only by the depth of interpersonal animosities. We feel the antagonisms to be of destructive intensity. Those involved might well consider they may hang together or they will hang separately."[240] After such a drubbing, other college administrators might have considered resignation. However, reflecting back on this admittedly difficult moment, Brother Mel later wrote in his memoirs: "Neither I nor my staff resigned nor did we lose heart."[241]

On the recommendation of the Academic Council, Brother Dominic proposed the appointment of a campus-wide Interpersonal Relations

Committee to investigate the acrimonious climate on campus. Introducing a note of levity into a grim environment, several faculty members began calling it the "Love Committee." After conducting numerous interviews and gathering considerable data, it released its findings in May 1977. It not only endorsed the recent WASC report but also went a step further by leveling especially strong criticisms of both the president and his academic vice-president. Although a few faculty members claimed that Brother Mel and Brother Dominic were being made "scapegoats" for the school's manifold problems, one-third of those interviewed spontaneously told committee members that Brother Mel should never have been named president, and half said that Brother Dominic should be removed from office.[242] Despite its frank tone, the committee's report came to be accepted by most members of the college community as a perceptive assessment of the hostile climate on campus and, what is more important, as a constructive guide for improving interpersonal relations. The administration strongly disagreed with this assessment and pretty much ignored the report's recommendations.

As soon as Brother Dominic took office, he began to expand the college's curriculum. The Academic Council approved new undergraduate majors in accounting, physical education and communications, and the administration opened negotiations with Merritt Hospital in Oakland for a new nursing program. On the graduate level, a new evening MBA program, several MA programs in education and MA programs in psychology and physical education were instituted, along with a paralegal certificate program. In 1975, Saint Mary's signed an agreement with the Institute for Professional Development (IPD) in San Jose to provide working adults with evening and weekend classes to complete their bachelor's degrees. Eventually, the institute moved its headquarters to Arizona, where it morphed into the gargantuan University of Phoenix. A year after signing with IPD, the college entered into a contractual agreement to establish an International Institute of Banking and Finance on campus, but it was soon discontinued because of a lack of institutional control. Many members of the undergraduate faculty claimed that these new programs did not fit into the liberal arts orientation of the college; one of them, modifying a phrase earlier coined by Robert Maynard Hutchins, claimed that Brother Dominic's educational gambits were "a series of unrelated activities held together by the plumbing system."

On the basis of complaints about the college's contract with IPD, WASC officials made a special "fact-finding" visit to Saint Mary's in May 1977, in advance of the scheduled follow-up visit set for October. The small team concluded that the school's extended education degree programs did not reflect the unique qualities of a Saint Mary's education.[243] When the larger "follow-up" WASC team arrived on campus in October 1977, it was concerned, therefore, not only with the holdover problems of weak finances and poor morale, highlighted two years earlier, but also with the new issues of the academic quality and institutional control of the external degree programs that had been initiated subsequent to that earlier visit. It criticized most of these new off-campus "contract" programs for being low in quality, loosely administered and insufficiently controlled by the college.[244] Early in 1978, WASC placed Saint Mary's College on "probation" until the next visit in 1980, while maintaining its full accreditation. Kay Anderson, the executive director of the agency, told Brother Mel that "the Commission took this action because of its judgment that there exists such a serious division of opinion among the trustees, administration, and faculty concerning institutional purposes and goals as to jeopardize the stability of the College and its capacity to maintain adequate controls over the quality of the programs."[245] Brother Dominic wanted to sue the accrediting agency, but Brother Mel agreed with some of its criticisms of the external degree programs.

Brother William Beatie Becomes Academic Vice-President

At the end of the spring term in 1978, Brother Dominic resigned from office. Brother Mel selected undergraduate dean Brother William Beatie to replace him because of his "meticulous clarity, [attention to detail], insight, [and] impatience with confusion."[246] The new AVP was not inclined to discard the educational programs that Brother Dominic had introduced because he shared his predecessor's desire to cater to "adult learners" and believed, in addition, that Saint Mary's needed to generate more revenue to support the expensive undergraduate college. However, he was determined to improve their quality and bring them under strict institutional control in order to satisfy WASC concerns.

In the fall of 1979, Dr. Robert J. Roxby was appointed director of the Extended Education Program on campus. When IPD failed to provide contracted services to students, he recommended sequestering funds that were owed to it. On February 14, 1980, IPD's head, Dr. John Sperling, complained in a letter to Saint Mary's that $12,544.25 had been held back for no good reason. Insisting that the college was exaggerating any inconvenience it had suffered from a recent office move, he plausibly argued that its hidden purpose was to terminate its contract with IPD. "I am aware that the WASC leadership has conditioned St. Mary's accreditation on the termination of the IPD/SMC contract," he confided. However, Sperling warned Saint Mary's that if it broke its contract with IPD, there would be significant legal consequences. "We estimate," he continued, "that the damage which the Institute will suffer will exceed $1,200,000."[247] Attempting to avoid legal action, the college's lawyer offered IPD a settlement that was roughly equivalent to what Saint Mary's would have had to pay in court for legal fees, and Sperling accepted the offer after tough negotiations. The final sum, which remains confidential information, was far less than the figure of $1.2 million in damages that Sperling had earlier projected.

In mid-March 1980, an eleven-person WASC visitation team arrived on campus. It was seeking to determine whether significant progress had been made in the areas of finance, interpersonal relations and, especially, control of external degree programs. The team was generally pleased with what it found. "Much has been accomplished since 1977," the final report concluded.[248] On the basis of a stronger financial picture, a friendlier atmosphere on campus and strengthened institutional control of extended education programs, among other things, the visiting team recommended that the college's "probationary" status be rescinded. On June 26, WASC's executive director informed Brother Mel that the commission had voted at its June 23–25 meeting to remove the college from probation.

During Brother William's tenure in office, significant changes were made to the undergraduate curriculum. As a former philosophy professor and a product of the Great Books Program, he was determined to return to the traditional World Classics Seminars that had been abandoned in 1969 during the SPAN revolution. This restoration took place in 1983. At about the same time, English composition courses and breadth requirements were also restored.

As Saint Mary's grew in size and complexity, adding several new undergraduate, graduate and extended degree programs, it became imperative to update its administrative structure. In 1985, Brother William made the Departments of Education and Extended Education Program into Schools, each headed by a dean. The former chairmen of the three undergraduate schools, who until that moment held impressive titles but exercised little real authority, now became full-fledged deans with commensurate jurisdiction over various academic departments.

In response to WASC recommendations, the college also instituted its first academic senate in the fall of 1988. It got off to a shaky start when its second chairman resigned the following year because he judged that neither the administration nor the faculty was sufficiently supportive of the new body. Overcoming its growing pains, the senate functioned more smoothly in later years.

DR. WILLIAM HYNES BECOMES ACADEMIC VICE-PRESIDENT

In the spring of 1990, after twelve years in office, Brother William Beatie decided to return to the classroom. Two search committees in two stages were appointed to select his successor. They finally settled on Dr. William J. Hynes, the academic dean of Regis University, a Jesuit institution in Denver. Hynes had earned his doctorate in the history of Christian thought at the University of Chicago in 1976. An active scholar, he had written or edited three books. Given his strong academic background, Hynes encouraged faculty research, secured

grants to invite Woodrow Wilson Fellows and Marshall Fellows to campus for lectures and sponsored summer workshops for the faculty on the liberal arts, Catholic higher education and the Lasallian heritage. He also established the "Professor of the Year" award, which includes a generous stipend and the opportunity to address the faculty on an important topic. One of Hynes's first actions was to create the office of director of faculty development. After a national search, Dr. Monica Hyde was selected for the position. Her mandate was to encourage better teaching and faculty scholarship.

English professor Robert Hass, Poet Laureate of the United States and MacArthur "Genius" Award recipient. *Courtesy of the Saint Mary's College Archives, Moraga.*

Some professors complained that the new AVP placed too

much emphasis on scholarly publications for promotion to full professor. His supporters contended that he believed that good teaching was dependent on keeping up in one's field and doing original research. In line with his emphasis on original scholarship, Dr. Hynes advocated the reduction of the faculty teaching load from seven to six courses. This would not only allow professors to engage in more scholarly research and writing but also permit them to interact more with their students. The problem here was the acute shortage of office space on campus. Reducing the teaching load was also intimately tied in with the question of whether or not to retain the 4-1-4 calendar. During the 1990–91 school year, following a mandate from the Board of Trustees, the academic senate seriously debated switching back to the older calendar arrangement of two fifteen-week semesters and no intersession. This change might have occurred if the administration had agreed to a six-course teaching load, but Brother Mel believed that such a move was not financially feasible.

Responding to national trends in higher education, AVP Hynes was able to secure more than $2 million from the James Irvine Foundation to enhance campus diversity in the recruitment of students, faculty and staff from minority backgrounds. Special admissions counselors were hired and programs developed to attract more minority professors and send more minority students on to graduate schools. Minority students with a proclivity for college teaching were awarded generous scholarships for their junior and senior years at the college and for their first two years of graduate school, on condition that they returned to teach at Saint Mary's for three years. Scholarships were also granted to alumni already in graduate school.

In the summer of 1987, the Board of Trustees passed a motion to ascertain how the college might improve its image with African Americans and Hispanics and increase the enrollment of students from these two minority groups. In the following year, Brother Mel appointed a sixteen-member task force, headed by Dean Paul Zingg of the School of Liberal Arts and advising dean Thomas Brown, to address these concerns. The final report contained a bold plan to significantly remake the college's admissions and financial aid policies and its curriculum, campus life and governance structures. When the chair of the faculty senate demanded that Brother Mel appear before the body to discuss the "Task Force Report on Minority Presence," he held back. Once again, the specter of student and faculty protests cast a dark shadow over the school, as a dangerous impasse seemed about to develop. Tensions rose when the academic senate voted 12–0 to endorse the report's sweeping recommendations as stated in the executive summary. Through the good offices of Dr. Hynes, four meetings were arranged between the task force and the president to smooth out differences. The resulting compromise, entitled "Celebrating Diversity," was presented to the senate in May 1991. Fortunately, a potential contretemps was thereby defused, and the years of tranquility, begun during Brother William's administration, continued.

Brother Mel's Tenure Comes to an End

In 1995, as Brother Mel's last four-year term as president was about to end, the Board of Trustees was asked to evaluate his performance and to recommend to the provincial whether or not he should be reappointed. After the requisite interviews were conducted, it favored reappointment until 1999. Brother Mel indicated at the time that this would be his last term in office, if confirmed. However, Brother Mark Murphy, the visitor at the time, decided to grant Brother Mel only two more years in office. His successor, Brother David Brennan, immediately informed the trustees of his plans to name a new president by July 1, 1997.[249]

Brother Mel's last meeting with the board in June 1997 was unsettling. The incoming new president, Brother Craig Franz, Brother David and board chair Brendan "B.J." Cassin questioned a contract that had been made between the college and William McLeod, who had been recently appointed vice-president for administration and chief financial officer. "In a divided but close vote," Brother Mel writes in his memoirs, "the Board, obviously under pressure from both the Chair and the Provincial, rescinded McLeod's contract. I left the meeting chagrined and disgusted, as did several other Board members."[250] Board of Trustees minutes in the college archives are not helpful in shedding light on this contretemps. Those of June 17, 1997, only indicate that "a confidential matter was discussed." After McLeod threatened to sue the college for breach of contract, he was later given a position in the Development Office and kept on as CFO until a replacement could be found.

In advance of this disturbing trustees' meeting, in April 1997 Brother Mel was given a rousing "send-off" by trustees, regents, alumni, faculty and friends in the grand ballroom of the Hilton Hotel in San Francisco. On that memorable evening of feasting and toasting, an endowed scholarship fund was created in his honor; it has since grown to over $1 million dollars. Brother Mel was also presented with a generous check that permitted him to sail on the Baltic Sea for ten days during the coming summer. If he reflected on his years as president while strolling on the cruise ship deck, he could have taken genuine satisfaction in having made important contributions to Saint Mary's. If growth is the measure, Brother Mel had been quite successful. During his long tenure, the faculty had increased from 135 to almost 300 and the student body from 950 to nearly 4,000. Brother Mel also left his successor not only with many beautiful buildings but also with financial stability, a revitalized curriculum, a strong athletic program, improved student services, a growing endowment and several generous benefactors. However, whether Saint Mary's became more Catholic and more devoted to the liberal arts after Brother Mel's twenty-eight years in office is not clear. At the end of his tenure, only 1 percent of the degrees granted were in philosophy and theology, and 49 percent were granted in business administration.

Chapter 13
A Promise Unfulfilled
··
The Presidency of Brother Craig Franz,
1997–2005

In late 1996, the provincial, Brother David Brennan, decided to involve the entire Saint Mary's College community in the selection of Brother Mel's successor. As a consequence, a broad-based, fourteen-person committee was appointed to conduct a national search. It finally settled on Brother Craig Franz of the Baltimore District. A former Fulbright Fellow, he held a doctorate in marine biology from the University of Rhode Island, had published twenty-two scholarly articles and had served in recent years as the assistant to the president of Saint Mary's University in Winona, Minnesota. A strikingly handsome, athletic and charming man, he began each day with a bracing morning swim.

Being an "outsider" was both an asset and a liability for Brother Craig as he assumed office. At the time of his appointment, a staff member commented that it was fortunate that the new president had come from elsewhere "because he'll bring a fresh, brand-new perspective."[251] Others on campus doubtless shared this hope. However, a couple years into his presidency, Brother Craig counted as one of his two major weaknesses "not having the exceedingly valued 'currency' afforded to those who hold a Saint Mary's diploma and/or are members of the San Francisco District of the Christian Brothers."[252]

According to Brother Craig, he tried to arrange an informal dinner meeting with his predecessor before arriving on campus. However, Brother Mel declined the invitation. "Walking into the [president's] office on that first day," Brother Craig recalls, "I encountered his keys and a sealed letter

Brother Craig Franz, president during the Pledge Scandal. *Courtesy of the Saint Mary's College Archives, Moraga.*

waiting on the desk for me." It urged the new president to curb the Board of Trustees and to steer clear of the Christian Brothers provincial. Doubtless, this advice reflected Brother Mel's displeasure with what had happened at his last board meeting. Reflecting on his first day on the job, Brother Craig later exclaimed, "It was quite a welcome!"[253]

To his credit, Brother Craig scheduled a series of coffee hours, fireside chats and town hall meetings to get to know the college community. However, a large number of faculty and staff members quickly concluded that these listening exercises offered the "appearance [but not the reality] of collaboration."[254] Perhaps unwisely, Brother Craig decided to surround himself with a small klatch of handpicked advisers, almost all of whom were from off campus and therefore "outsiders" like himself. Among them were Christian Brother Jack Curran from the New York District, appointed vice-president of student affairs; Dr. James Devine, formerly of La Salle University in Philadelphia, appointed assistant to the president; and attorney Marianne Schimelfenig, appointed as the college's first chief counsel. These three advisors, especially "Jim and Marianne," formed the president's tight inner circle, which was not easy to penetrate.

Faculty members were pleased with a number of the new president's early actions, including increasing the technology budget, reducing the teaching load from seven to six courses a year and approving more faculty sabbaticals. Unfortunately, Brother Craig's early constructive moves did not bring him the popularity and respect he might have reasonably expected. To many on campus, these initiatives seemed tactical, conditioned and insufficiently funded rather than components of an overall plan to improve the academic atmosphere on campus.

Two Mid-Term Presidential Evaluations

A year after taking office, in some "reflections" for the alumni magazine, Brother Craig underscored his desire to respond to what he regarded as a new and promising educational constituency of older, adult learners seeking better jobs or brighter futures. In line with this thinking, Brother Craig later instituted several new external degree, certificate, on-line and graduate programs. Many members of the undergraduate faculty, devoted to the ideal of a small residential liberal arts college, greeted Brother Craig's new programs with apprehension and even disapproval. As during the administration of Brother Dominic, it was widely believed that they were being initiated for their revenue-producing potential rather than for their intrinsic educational value. For his part, Brother Craig sincerely believed he was only being Lasallian.

There were many other areas of discontent. Top academic administrators objected to what they regarded as the president's tendency to micro-manage and his "mindless" cost-cutting policies,[255] and staff members complained of wrongful termination and of their inability to lodge justified grievances for fear of retribution.[256] Students were also disgruntled. In the spring of 1998, a group staged a "Take Back the Night" march to demand better lighting on campus against the threat of sexual assault. Although Brother Craig came out to talk to the protestors gathered in front of the chapel, to their dismay he read from a prepared statement written by the college's new marketing director. Student discontent boiled over again late in 1999, when a group of protestors gathered in the plaza in front of the chapel under the founder's imposing bronze statue to rail against the new president;

they complained of, in particular, an "out of touch" administration, Brother Craig's unpopular decision not to live with them in the dormitories and, as is oftentimes the case in student protests, inedible food in the cafeteria. One student forlornly held up a handmade sign that read simply: "Brother Craig you are a disappointment."[257]

Because Brother Craig's first two and a half years in office were troubled, the Board of Trustees initiated a presidential evaluation process in the fall of 1999, a full year and a half before his contract was up for renewal. After numerous meetings and interviews, an investigatory committee concluded that the new president had acted more like a "manager" than a "leader" during his first years as president, citing in support of this conclusion his "lack of articulation of vision; lack of presence and interaction on campus; failure to hear, reflect and respond; inadequate direct reports; lack of compassion and guidance in bureaucracy; [and] need to be more interactive with the Brothers."[258] At about the same time, an independent Academic Administrators Evaluation Committee painted a darker, more disparaging portrait of the inexperienced new president.

As part of the trustee evaluation process, Brother Craig submitted an eighteen-page presidential self-evaluation. Among the personal weaknesses he confessed to was "not being able to put things behind me, develop a thick skin, and sleep uninterruptedly through the night."[259] This statement would indicate that all of the turmoil of his early years in office had exacted a high emotional and physic toll on the young administrator and that those who claimed that Brother Craig was unfazed by the problems and troubles he initially encountered were almost certainly wrong.

Notwithstanding a torrent of criticism, the Board of Trustees decided not to ask for Brother Craig's resignation but to give him more time to prove himself. However, several on the faculty itself were not as sanguine about the president's prospects for improvement. One full-time professor told the Academic Administrators Evaluation Committee: "I simply don't think it's possible. Let me put it a different way: I don't think this particular President can make such a change in himself or in his style and management. He's gone too far."[260]

Although Brother Craig remained in office, his AVP did not. Early in 2000, the Board of Trustees discharged Dr. Hynes. He and the president had been at loggerheads for some time, but this action came as an unpleasant surprise to many in the academic community. In the spring, psychology professor Sarah "Sally" Stampp of the Psychology Department was appointed interim academic vice-president. She was widely known and respected on campus as a capable instructor and a calm personality. However, some faculty members objected when the president later made her interim appointment permanent, without a further in-house or national search.

J.C. GATEHOUSE HALL

In October 1997, Brother Craig launched the "Spirit of Saint Mary's" fundraising campaign, with the goal of collecting $75 million. A year later, this figure was raised to $150 million and then, two years later, to a stupendous $190 million, after two anonymous donors pledged $121 million. Today we know who both of these men are. One was Conrad Colbrandt, a middle-aged man, dapper and mustached, who headed a Walnut Creek mortgage brokerage firm, Tracol Limited and Forefront Properties. The other was Colbrandt's close associate, John Slade Banker, a deeply wrinkled, balding man in his late

Science School faculty at the J.C. Gatehouse Hall groundbreaking. *Courtesy of the Saint Mary's College Archives, Moraga.*

seventies and the nephew of the cofounder of Coldwell Banker Real Estate Company. Neither Colbrandt nor Banker had graduated from Saint Mary's College or had family connections with or any other ties to the institution.

Seemingly awash in money, the Saint Mary's Development Office began drawing up plans to construct a large number of significant new buildings. On this list, a new science building was given top priority. On November 17, 1998, groundbreaking took place in the Poplar Grove where Brother Craig had been inaugurated during elaborate ceremonies that some had compared to a coronation. Both of the anonymous donors were in attendance, although their identities remained hidden to all but a select few. It was announced at this time that the new science center would be called "J.C. Gatehouse" Hall. This strange name, designed to preserve and protect the anonymity of the two donors, became a subject of widespread speculation on campus. The construction of the new facility was put on the fast track because of the obvious need for it and because of fears of steadily rising construction costs. Although the anonymous donors had put their pledges in writing, they kept delaying the actual payment, usually for tax reasons. To bridge the financing for the new science center, the college dipped into reserve funds and took out loans from the Bank of America.

Controversial J.C. Gatehouse Hall. *Courtesy of the Saint Mary's College Archives, Moraga.*

Brother Craig's Second Term

Despite continuing student protests, now over the issue of date rape on campus, and two extremely negative evaluations, the Board of Trustees granted Brother Craig a second four-year term, beginning on June 30, 2001. Two years later, the president announced that AVP Stampp would assume the additional title of provost and take charge of all academic and student affairs. This new governance model enabled Brother Craig to spend more time off campus in spreading the Lasallian educational message in this country and abroad. In 2003, he became the first president of the International Association of Lasallian Universities, a consortium of sixty-five Christian Brothers' colleges and universities around the world.

In November 2003, Brother Craig created an eighteen-member Athletic Review Task Force and charged it with taking a hard look at how the school's limited sports budget was being allocated. After several months of meetings and interviews, it came to the unanimous conclusion that Saint Mary's could not become competitive on the gridiron without offering as many as forty or fifty additional football scholarships but that the school could not afford this further outlay. It would make more sense, it concluded, to transfer the money spent on football, approximately $1.2 million out of a total athletic budget of nearly $7 million, to other sports in order to make them more competitive with West Coast Conference schools with larger enrollments and larger athletic budgets but no costly football team to subsidize.

The reaction to the dropping of football on campus was mixed. Understandably, both the players and their coaches felt misled and betrayed. One former player told the *Contra Costa Times*: "I always thought Saint Mary's was about helping people, about being Christian leaders, about honoring values and traditions. If this is a representation of what Lasallian values are, then I'm ashamed to be a Gael."[261] Most regular students took the decision to discontinue football in stride or actually applauded it. A junior from Santa Cruz commented: "I went to one game my freshman year and there was no energy in the stadium. It was a joke. They were losing, and they were cocky. A lot of my friends were happy the football team was cut."[262] Some on campus hoped that reallocating resources would help make basketball the marquee sport and put the school back on the athletic map.

The Pledge Scandal

In late January 2004, Brother Stanislaus Campbell, who had succeeded Brother David as visitor, announced that Brother Craig had "enthusiastically" accepted appointment to a third term. The provincial specifically commended the president for instituting the provost model of governance and for diversifying the student body.[263] Brother Raphael Patton, a member of the 1999 Trustee Presidential Evaluation Committee, believes that Brother Craig's "re-appointment was due entirely (I am guessing here, but it is not a thoughtless guess) to the affliction of the District fearing to replace an administrator. He is there, nothing terrible has happened, and so he stays on. It kept [Brother] Mel in place for [nearly] 30 years!"[264] The problem was that something quite "terrible" was about to happen shortly into Brother Craig's third term.

In August 2004, Conrad Colbrandt abruptly informed college officials that the large and numerous pledges he and John Slade Banker had made since 1997 would not be redeemed. They had been based, he divulged, on two cunning but fraudulent real estate schemes involving the sale, relocation and leasing of PepsiCo fast-food franchises. In late July or early August, Banker, now eighty-four years old, abandoned his car and apartment and absconded to Mexico with between $4 and $9 million that he had bilked from 110 groups and 200 individual investors in California, Hawaii, Oregon, Nevada, Colorado, Texas, Indiana and Tennessee.[265] In the summer of 2004, his criminal past was finally brought to light. Crime records revealed that he had been arrested in 1979 and charged with forty-three counts of grand theft and forgery in connection with a Bay Area real estate scheme to sell restaurant properties he did not actually own. Convicted a year after his arrest, Banker was sentenced in 1980 to five years in state prison.[266] Colbrandt, who was forced to resign from the Board of Regents, claimed that he was as much a victim of Banker's scams as the unfortunate investors who had lost their pants and the Saint Mary's officials who had lost their pledges.[267]

In an e-mail letter to the college community, dated August 13, 2004, Brother Craig and new board chairman Nicholas Moore claimed that the school had been the victim of "a serious act of deception" and that the promised pledges would therefore not be finally "forthcoming."[268] The shocked trustees immediately set up a three-man special committee to look into the whole sad affair. Its triple mandate was to ascertain the facts and circumstances surrounding the default on the pledges, to determine if any of the college's fundraising and construction policies had been violated and to recommend "corrective measures" so that something of this nature would never happen again.[269]

The seventy-eight-page "Report by the Special Committee Regarding the Failed Anonymous Pledges" was released to the public on October 14, 2004. A murder mystery could not have spun a more intriguing story of forged documents, criminal impersonations, counterfeit business cards and elaborate but plausible con jobs. The report basically exonerated Brother Craig, the Development Office and the board of any intentional or criminal wrongdoing, concluding that prior to August 2004 no one at Saint Mary's knew that the pledges were bogus and that there had been no violation of the college's policy requiring written pledges before beginning construction on new buildings. However, certain serious deficiencies in procedures were identified by the report, and it was determined that "greater diligence and better communication" on campus might have exposed the deception sooner.[270] In short, the college should never have begun construction on the new science center without having some money in hand, and it should have conducted thorough background searches on both Colbrandt and Banker.

Because the trustee-commissioned report, which was really more of a Power Point presentation, did not consider the caper's human dimension, it fell to newspaper reports, locally and in New York City, to offer commentary on personal motivations and failures. For example, the *San Francisco Chronicle* tried to explain the genesis of the scandal by highlighting Brother Craig's inexperience and the rah-rah attitude of the Board of Trustees. "Everything was just perfect for a scam," Dr. Lionel Chan, the former college CFO, was quoted as saying. "You have a new president—he's young and inexperienced and gung-ho. You have a board that wants to support the president and wants him to act as a president…The president had these great ideas about starting new."[271] Expanding on this idea, Chan told the *New York Times* that Brother Craig "was given the benefit of the doubt because he was new and people wanted him to succeed."[272] In the *Contra Costa Times*, Dean Keith Devlin of the School of Science also chalked up the pledge scandal to youth and hubris: "[Brother] Craig was young. It was his first presidency…I think his ambition got the better of him."[273]

When all is said and done, it appears that there are three main reasons why Saint Mary's College was hoodwinked: the inexperience and overreaching of its new president, the failure of its Development Office to practice due diligence and the failure of the Board of Trustees to seek more information on the pledges. The website of the Walnut Creek Police Department indicates that Banker is still a wanted man and has never been apprehended. His cold case number is 04-20775, and anyone with knowledge of his whereabouts is urged to call Detective Craig Leonard. Most likely, Banker is enjoying the high life in Mexico, if he is still alive.

Two Resignations

After the scandal broke, Brother Craig tendered his resignation, effective January 1, 2005. No other member of the college administration followed suit. "It has become clear to me," Brother Craig confessed to the campus community on September 21, "that evolving perceptions about my leadership would make it increasingly difficult for me to effectively inspire our alumni and others to support the College now and in the future. I am stepping aside now because my paramount interest is seeing Saint Mary's move forward."[274] In a letter to the college community, board chairman Moore insisted that he had tried to talk Brother Craig out of resigning. Expressing "profound appreciation" for Brother Craig's fine leadership of the college, he listed among his achievements a threefold increase in the college's endowment, which was a real accomplishment, and the construction of the new science center, which was later named in honor of Brother Alfred Brousseau.[275] In another communication to the Saint Mary's community, written three months later, Moore changed his tone and admitted that Brother Craig had been a controversial president. During his time in office, "some faculty members questioned the level of commitment by administrators to shared governance. There was staff concern about the level of sensitivity shown to departing colleagues. As a consequence of a thoughtful, in-depth examination of our Athletics program, football was discontinued. Most recently, we all faced the unanticipated and painful realization that a series of significant financial pledges would not be realized."[276]

While gratefully acknowledging Brother Craig's acceptance of personal responsibility by resigning, the academic senate passed a formal resolution on October 7, 2005, asking the Board of Trustees to "formally acknowledge its own responsibility in all matters related to the unrealized pledge, including its impact on the future of the College."[277] In response, Moore admitted to "failed opportunities" in detecting the fraud, a lack of "sufficient communication" among and with the trustees and inadequate "oversight" in the "planning and construction process." "Just as the report affirms that Saint Mary's was a victim of deception," he added, "it also makes clear that we could, and should, have done many things differently."[278]

By resigning, Brother Craig clearly manifested the personal integrity that several faculty members had earlier doubted he had ever possessed. The editorial writer of the *Contra Costa Times* characterized Brother Craig "as a man of honor" for his action.[279] The former president later confided that he was willing to fall on the proverbial sword because the college needed to get over the trauma of the pledge scandal as quickly as possible.[280]

A year into a national search for a new president of Saint Mary's University in Winona, Brother Craig submitted a late application. He easily beat out one other candidate. However, a year and a half later, Brother Craig resigned for a second time, after it was revealed that he had had a "sexual encounter" in Moraga with a Saint Mary's student after he announced his resignation following the fundraising scandal but before he actually left campus. When informed of this incident by the affected student, whose identity was never revealed, Brother Craig's successor as president, Brother Ronald Gallagher, contacted Christian Brother officials in the Saint Louis and Baltimore Districts regarding the allegation and ordered an independent investigation. Confronted with the results of this inquiry by the chairman of the Saint Mary's University Board of Trustees, Brother Craig confessed to sexual behavior "inappropriate" for a Christian Brother under vows and a college president, "leader, teacher, and mentor."[281] "I am sure it is as troubling to you as it is to me that one of our students was subjected to improper sexual conduct," Brother Ronald told the Saint Mary's community in a December letter informing it of the sad incident. Apparently no other students were involved,[282] and it should be emphasized that the individual involved was an adult and not a minor. Back at the Moraga campus, the student body president remarked, in light of both the pledge scandal and the recent revelation of sexual impropriety, "It has been a bit of a rough run. It will be interesting, come January, to see what morale is like."[283]

Brother Craig's Administration: An Assessment

In retrospect, Brother Craig frankly admits that his time at Saint Mary's "was a difficult one" for the campus, for the faculty and for himself. We have already documented the discontent, mishaps and scandals that marred his administration. However, it would be a mistake to leave the impression that nothing of value happened during his tenure in office. There were a number of positive developments that should be mentioned here, including balancing the annual budget, growing the college's endowment and increasing financial aid. When Brother Craig left the presidency, Saint Mary's was in sound financial condition. Another major achievement was improving technology on campus, although there are those who would disagree with the manner in which this worthy goal had been pursued. During Brother Craig's two terms, several physical improvements were made, including the erection of a badly needed science center, a new performing arts center and the completion of a remodeled and enlarged student union. Although the college ended up paying for the new science building from its own resources, its erection was probably worth the scandal that had attended it. At the dedication ceremony, Brother Craig asked longtime biology professor Lawrence Cory, "Did you ever expect to see such a magnificent structure as this on the Saint Mary's campus?" He replied, "I've been dreaming about this for forty-nine years."[284] Perhaps Brother Craig's signature accomplishment, apart from construction projects, was discontinuing the football program and channeling funds to other athletic programs to make them more competitive in the West Coast Conference. This strategy has proved a brilliant success, as both men's and women's teams have become dominant in recent years.

The great tragedy of Brother Craig's administration was not a lack of good will or of a coherent educational vision; rather, it resulted from the wrong man being placed in the wrong place at the wrong time. As several faculty members remarked in different ways, "He is very good at something we don't want."[285] Brother Craig wanted to break open the school by pushing it in new experimental educational directions, whereas most of the undergraduate faculty wanted it to remain a small residential liberal arts college. Presently, Brother Craig resides at the Christian Brothers motherhouse in Rome, where he coordinates two foundations that provide financial assistance to worthy Lasallian operations in Third World countries. The troubles of the years have aged him, and he looks wane and gaunt, although he still swims regularly and even wins prizes.

Chapter 14

A Time of Restoration

·······························

The Presidency of Brother Ronald Gallagher, 2005–2013

As soon as Brother Craig announced his resignation, the search for his successor began in earnest. He was Brother Ronald Gallagher, chairman of the English and Drama Department. Brother Ronald had been the leading candidate in 1997, when Brother Craig had unexpectedly gotten the nod, and he was not to be overlooked for a second time. Brother Ronald's formal inauguration took place on September 23, 2005, in the plaza area in front of the chapel.

His speech was reminiscent of President Warren G. Harding's benign call in 1921 for "restoration" not "revolution." A year after Brother Ronald's inauguration, a new Board of Trustees chairman, Ray Larkin,

Brother Ronald Gallagher, president from 2005 to 2013. *Courtesy of the Saint Mary's College Archives.*

reiterated this call for a return to tradition and tranquility in an interview for the alumni magazine. "What has pleased me the most has been to see the College return to its core values," he told the executive editor. "For years, the College was focused on mending fences and fixing problems."[286]

Strengthening the Catholic Core

By far, the most provocative comments during the inaugural week celebrations were delivered by Dr. Don Biel, Koch Chair of Catholic Studies at the University of Saint Thomas in Minnesota. He mentioned that there were five principal obstacles confronting any Catholic college or university, including Saint Mary's, that would attempt to honor and advance the Catholic intellectual tradition: the "emotivism" (one suspects this means how one "feels" about things) of increasing numbers of undergraduates; the strength and autonomy of the various academic disciplines; the "fundamental agnosticism of the academy"; the "loss of conviction that either faith or reason has truth as its object"; and "the prevalence of a technological culture" that tends to "instrumentalize all aspects of human life."[287] Many of these trends might be discerned at Saint Mary's College, where the reigning spirit on campus in recent decades had become more pluralistic and less formally religious.

Perhaps to avoid the creation by conservative professors of a competing Catholic studies major based on a similar program at Saint Thomas University, the Religious Studies Department preemptively introduced in the fall of 2006 a new minor concentration in the Catholic tradition, requiring students to complete six courses in various fields such as church history, Catholic social teaching and the Catholic imagination. Religious studies professor and former Christian Brother Dr. Paul Giurlanda, the chief spokesman for the new minor, commented to the alumni magazine, "Even though we feel a student can get a good education in Catholicism, we decided maybe we needed to be more explicit."[288]

In an allied effort to strengthen the institution's Catholic character, Brother Michael Sanderl, the only young brother on campus with a doctorate, was named in the fall of 2007 the college's first dean of campus ministry. His mandate was to enrich the liturgical experience on campus and deepen the spirituality of the students. However, after a short time in office, he left the Christian Brothers congregation to get married, pursuing a path that numerous other confreres have also beaten since Vatican II. Brother Michael's departure probably heightened expectations that the next president of Saint Mary's College would be a layperson.

Dropping Extended Education

On May 20, 2005, only months after Brother Ronald took office, the Board of Trustees made a momentous decision. Based on a recommendation of an ad hoc team of faculty, staff and administrators, it voted to end admissions to the School of Extended Education (SEED), after negotiations to transfer certain external degree programs to Regis University in Denver broke down. For several decades, SEED had produced a steady, sometimes even gushing, revenue stream for the college. Founding dean Robert Roxby attributes the school's demise to a series of poor administrative decisions. The curriculum had been resigned, he claims, to "occupy formats that were not appropriate for the education of adults." The library generously responded to the needs of these new learners, but the financial aid and registrar's offices did not, in his opinion. Increasing competition from the fast-growing University of Phoenix also had adverse effects on the college's external degree program. The *San Francisco Business Times* forthrightly declared, "Blame it [the phase-out of the Saint Mary's program] on a glutted industry."[289] Additionally, multiplying learning centers at a considerable distance from the Moraga campus turned out to be ill advised, leading to increasing costs and a lack of quality control. In retrospect, Brother Mel sees another "angle" to the elimination of SEED. He contends that the School of Economics and Business Administration (SEBA) was opposed to continuing the extended education program because the American Association of College Schools of Business would not grant its accreditation to an institution with a large adjunct faculty teaching in a business program over which SEBA did not exercise direct control.[290] Finally, it is important to note that from SEED's founding in 1975, there had always been a significant segment of the faculty opposed to its very existence on philosophical grounds. The phase-out of extended education programs, including paralegal and law studies, suggests that Brother Mel's earlier claim that Brother Dominic's programs had changed the very "destiny" of the college was not valid.[291]

As might be expected, the demise of the Extended Education School left problems in its wake. In order to upgrade the program and ameliorate

WASC concerns, a number of full-time, tenure-track professors had been hired over the years. Following AAUP rules, once SEED was suppressed, positions had to be found or created for these displaced faculty members in the college's regular undergraduate and graduate programs. According to a respected, longtime faculty member, this process has been "sometimes acrimonious and often wrenching."[292]

With SEED removed from the academic scene, Saint Mary's College placed more emphasis on celebrating and strengthening its undergraduate curriculum. In the fall of 2006, the Integral Program marked its fiftieth anniversary with a yearlong celebration. In January 2009, it added to its laurels by obtaining accreditation from the American Academy for Liberal Education. It was now placed in the same prestigious category as other Great Books colleges in the United States, such as the two campuses of Saint John's College in Annapolis and Santa Fe and Thomas Aquinas College near Santa Paula. In the fall of 2005, some thirty-five years after female students arrived on campus, Saint Mary's College finally offered its first women's studies major; a minor had been established in 1993. By now, fully 60 percent of the undergraduate enrollment was made up of female students; the putative "Mother of Men" had now become the actual "Mother [mainly] of Women." Three years later, in 2008, the academic senate approved a new ethnic studies minor, which sought to provide multiple perspectives on gender, class, religion, race and ethnicity.

A New Provost Makes Important Academic Changes

In the fall of 2007, provost and vice-president for academic affairs Sara "Sally" Stampp announced that she would be returning to her teaching position in the Psychology Department. After a comprehensive national search, Dr. Bethami "Beth" Dobkin was named her successor in February of the following year. Extroverted, candid and energetic, she cuts a different figure from the more unhurried and methodical Stampp. A native Northern Californian with a doctorate in rhetoric and social order from the University of Massachusetts, Dobkin had been teaching in the Department of Communications Studies at the University of San Diego for the past seventeen years. Since 2005, she had served as the institution's associate provost.

In 2011, the academic senate reformulated the common curriculum that all students are required to take by stressing learning objectives. Perhaps of even greater import, it also modified the World Classics Seminars (or Collegiate Seminars, as they are now called) initiated during World War II by Professor Hagerty and resurrected by Dr. Slakey and Brother William. In his inaugural address, Brother Ronald had claimed that he had "heard from numerous alumni that what they value most from the Saint Mary's education is the great books seminar experience, which has made them thoughtful and articulate citizens, and given them a broad vision and a critical mind."[293] Nonetheless, both the faculty and academic senate voted to partially abandon the requirement of four seminars based on the chronological reading of the Great Books of the Western World. The new program, dubbed Model Three, includes a spring (not fall) freshman seminar on "Critical Strategies and Great Questions," based on short, targeted readings, both contemporary and classical, that are judged to be "accessible" and "relevant"; on a fall sophomore seminar on the Greek and Latin Worlds; a junior year seminar based on readings from the Renaissance through the year 1900; and a senior seminar on "The Global Conversation of the 20th and 21st Centuries," based on texts from world cultures and including a capstone experience.[294] In light of

A Great Books Seminar. *Courtesy of the Saint Mary's College Archives, Moraga.*

these recent changes, it seems fair to conclude that the claim that Saint Mary's College makes about being an institution devoted historically to the Great Books has been somewhat compromised, even though students will continue to take four seminars and read common texts, mostly from the Western World in two seminars, over their four-year academic careers. An alumnus of the college recently commented that it is ironic that Brother Ronald, "an Integral graduate and a lover of James Joyce, [would] preside over and [apparently] agree with the decision to marginalize the Great Books, rhetoric notwithstanding."[295] One could argue in support of the recent changes that they constitute a long overdue response to WASC concerns about the efficacy of the Seminar Program and to persistent student complaints, first voiced some forty years earlier.

Late in the spring term of 2012, the faculty engaged in a lively discussion of calendar and course credit changes proposed by a three-person task force committee of the academic senate. One of its members, philosophy professor Steven Cortright, convincingly showed that the credit requirements of Saint Mary's College, even if both the fall and spring terms were lengthened, would fall short of the equivalent 128 Carnegie units it was claiming that its thirty-six-course graduation requirement carried.[296] Because of a directive from the federal Department of Education, certain to be enforced by WASC, some reform of the current course credit system at Saint Mary's, however minimal, became inevitable. The big question facing the academic senate was whether to go long or to go short; that is, whether to discard the current calendar in favor of another, most likely two regular semesters with courses of variable unit values, or simply to tinker with the 4-1-4 system of the SPAN era in order to bring it more in compliance with accepted Carnegie unit computations. This could be accomplished either by lengthening the fall and spring terms or by increasing the number of minutes of a typical class hour. In the fall of 2012, the senate, working with a model created by Dr. Carl Guarneri of the History Department, decided to slightly shorten each term but increase class time from sixty to sixty-five minutes for three-day-a-week classes and from ninety to one hundred minutes for two-day-a-week classes. In terms of transfer units, typical Saint Mary's students would now accumulate roughly the equivalent of 126 units over four years, as opposed to the current, but unwarranted, claim of 128. Elaborate, and sometimes hard to follow, rationales were mounted in defense of the above option, also dubbed Model Three, but likely the real reason for its passage was that it was the least disruptive and the least expensive among other alternatives.

The provost, Dr. Dobkin, gave her approval for these various class period and unit changes, while reducing the time allotted for Tuesday-Thursday classes to ninety-five minutes.

THE WILLIAM AYERS CONTROVERSY

During the January term of 2009, the controversial educational theorist Professor William Ayers was scheduled to address the students and faculty of Saint Mary's College on the topic of "Trudging Toward Freedom: Building a Movement and Living Our Lives for Peace and Justice." Although Dr. Ayers was then serving as a professor in the Education Department of the University of Illinois in Chicago, he had earlier been one of the founders of the Weather Underground, a revolutionary group that opposed the war in Vietnam in the turbulent 1960s by setting off bombs in public buildings. Certain members of the Saint Mary's College community objected to Ayers's impending visit, regarding him as a former domestic terrorist. A group calling itself "Concerned Saint Mary's Students" asked other students and the college's donors to protest Ayers's appearance on campus. In an open letter, it declared, "Let's uphold the strong Lasallian Tradition that has distinguished Saint Mary's and its students for generations."[297] Under intense pressure to rescind the invitation proffered earlier, Brother Ronald instead decided to issue a thoughtful statement setting out the college's official position on the controversy. He judged that the Ayers lecture should go on as scheduled; to cancel it, the president declared, "would be to undermine the educational principles and values upon which our College is based…As a College with a Great Books tradition, we have a responsibility to defend the rights of those with controversial viewpoints to speak."[298] Despite outside protests and frequent interruptions, Ayers delivered his speech.

THE DIVERSITY QUESTION AND WASC

Shortly after taking office on March 1, 2005, Brother Ronald received a disturbing letter from Ralph A. Wolff, executive director of the WASC, based on the results of a periodic team visit that had taken place during October of the previous year when Brother Craig was still president. Among other things, Wolff stated that adult and graduate programs were still being regarded as "step children," that library funding remained inadequate, that a recommended "systematic evaluation" of the Collegiate Seminar Program had not taken place and that the new education doctorate program was so deficient that it should cease admitting students until an in-depth review could be completed. Even more troublesome, the visiting team, the letter stated, had witnessed "rude and disrespectful behavior to staff, faculty, and students of color," raising serious questions regarding the institution's commitment to fostering diversity and respect for persons.[299] To further look into these problem areas, the accrediting agency scheduled two upcoming visits.

After the WASC visit in October 2007, Wolff sent the college an action letter in the following February. It contained a "formal notice of concern" regarding the new doctoral program in educational leadership, library resources, graduate and adult education, the climate on campus and, most especially, the lack of respect for diversity. As for this last matter, the visiting team concluded that Saint Mary's had done a lot of "brainstorming" but that "tangible results" were still lacking. All campus constituencies, from the Board of Trustees on down, had not done enough to create "a culture of respect, civility, and cultural competency in keeping with the institution's own Lasallian core principles." Warning the college that it had to make real, tangible efforts to create a civil and respectful atmosphere on campus, Wolff bluntly stated that the agency was quite "prepared to issue a sanction," if necessary, for not complying with one of its key standards—namely, that "the institution's leadership creates and sustains a leadership system at all levels marked by high performance, appropriate responsibility, and accountability."[300]

The 2009 WASC visiting team fortunately found commendable progress on campus, beginning with the shaky doctoral program. It was also encouraged that Saint Mary's was finally making the library "central to its academic culture" by adding more personnel and more resources but pointed to continuing problems stemming from an acute lack of space. WASC also commended the college for doing a better job of integrating graduate and adult programs into the governance structures and educational mission of the institution. Finally, the team was encouraged by the appointment of a College Committee on Inclusive Excellence, the hiring of a human relations consultant and the positive attitude of the new provost on the diversity issue. "There has been a sincere effort resulting in substantial progress but much remains to be done," the final report stated, notwithstanding "the phenomenal efforts of the past two years."[301] Until the advent of Dr. Dobkin, it seemed as if the lessons learned from previous in-house and accreditation reports on the hostile climate on campus had been brushed aside rather than taken deeply to heart.

THE RISE AND FALL OF BASKETBALL

The college's various athletic teams excelled during Brother Ronald's presidency. Women's volleyball, men's and women's soccer, women's tennis, cross country, rugby and men's golf all achieved local and even national prominence from 2005 to 2010. However, it was the men's basketball team, under coach Randy Bennett, that garnered the greatest acclaim across the nation and even "down under" in Australia, the home of several of its star players. The 2009–10 basketball season was the best in the school's history. After beating perennial champion Gonzaga in the conference tournament in Las Vegas, the Gaels were invited once again to the "Big Dance," as the NCAA tournament is commonly called. After stunning upsets of both the University of Richmond and Villanova University, the team made it all the way to the select "Sweet Sixteen" before finally losing badly to Baylor University.

In the summer of 2012, the National Collegiate Athletic Association opened a full-scale investigation of the Saint Mary's men's basketball program. Because of delays, its report was not ready until the spring of 2013. On March 1, Brother Ronald informed the campus community of both the charges and the subsequent penalties that had been leveled. He noted that a former Gael assistant coach had offered "impermissible benefits" to recruits and that the team had engaged in "impermissible off-season training sessions." More seriously, head coach Bennett had failed to promote "an atmosphere of compliance" on campus. Because of these infractions, Saint Mary's was deprived of athletic scholarships, the head coach was suspended for five games at the start of the 2013–14 season and the Athletic Department was placed on probation for four years. "This is certainly a disappointing day for all of us who care so deeply about Saint Mary's," Brother Ronald confessed. The president went on to honestly admit that Saint Mary's was not "perfect." However, he was confident it would become "stronger" as it coped with and finally emerged from its impending ordeal. Although the college would accept "the findings" of the

NCAA report, Brother Ronald indicated that it might seek an appeal on the penalties. Nonetheless, he insisted that "our institution was founded on the principles of integrity, justice and Catholic values and challenges to those ideals will not be tolerated."[302] Later, Saint Mary's decided to appeal the penalties imposed by the NCAA.

As one might have expected, Brother Ronald's letter was as optimistic as possible in tone; the president even had a good word for Coach Bennett, characterizing him as "an outstanding representative of the College for more than 10 years."[303] ESPN Sports writer Andy Katz provided the best explanation of why Saint Mary's did not come down hard on Bennett: "He has had universal support at the school because men's basketball is the money sport and the one that has given the school a name." But then employing a faulty modifier, Katz issued a warning: "By sticking with him going forward, Bennett will have to repair his and the school's image by winning without any more drama."[304] There may be another reason why Bennett was not reprimanded. One of Brother Ronald's proudest achievements as president, in addition to expanding service learning, had been the remarkable success of the school's athletic programs. He confessed as much when he told a local newspaper that "as an alum, as president and someone who supports our athletic program, I'm…proud of what we have been able to accomplish…"[305]

Basketball experts believe that the Gaels will have another good season in 2013–14 because of the "horses already in the stable" but that the future of basketball at Saint Mary's remains murky at best. Perhaps the golden age of the last twelve years is about to pass into history. If upheld, the NCAA sanctions will make it difficult for Saint Mary's to recruit, train and develop talented players, and the lack of preseason tournament play will mean that the Gaels will not have the opportunity to play marquee schools in order to raise their profile. The temporary ban on games overseas may inhibit a program that relies heavily on recruiting foreign players. Despite a small budget, a cracker box gymnasium, the lack of a "national brand" and a limited fan base, Saint Mary's has been able to keep abreast of powerhouses Gonzaga University and Brigham Young University. As one sportswriter puts it, "Now the Gaels will also have to overcome scholarship, scheduling, and player development restrictions too."[306] It remains to be seen if they will be able to do that.

THE FIRST LAY PRESIDENT

Dr. James A. Donohue, first lay president.
Courtesy of the Saint Mary's College Archives, Moraga.

After serving for two terms, Brother Ronald decided he would not seek a third. After expressing gratitude for his achievements as president during trying times, the provincial, Brother Donald Johanson, announced a search process for his successor involving the use of headhunters. Significantly, he indicated that if a qualified Christian Brother could not be found, "then other practicing Catholic applicants will be invited to apply." On March 26, 2013, the visitor and the chairman of the Board of Trustees announced that Dr. James A. Donahue, the head of the Graduate Theological Union in Berkeley, would become the twenty-ninth president of Saint Mary's College. As a transition figure, Donahue was a reassuring choice: he was a practicing Catholic, a Jesuit graduate, a former Santa Clara professor, a theologian and an experienced administrator. Most important, he publicly professed deference to the Christian Brothers and their Lasallian heritage. As an added bonus, while serving as a vice-president for student affairs at Georgetown, Donahue had supervised a Division I athletic program, including compliance with NCAA policies and procedures. Even more fortuitously, he had served as longtime commissioner of WASC, the accrediting agency that has periodically tangled with Saint Mary's over a variety of issues.[307] Donahue was therefore perfectly positioned to address as an insider two serious problem areas at the college. If Donahue's curriculum vitae were not enough to allay fears of change, his physical appearance would probably suffice. He looks like an archetypical college president—with a narrow, scholarly face, an avuncular smile and a shock of white hair that makes him appear older than he actually is. His friendly manner and ready smile put everyone at ease.

An Uncertain Future

On October 6, 2012, a stunning early fall day, between five and seven thousand students, professors, alumni and friends of the college and their families gathered on the beautiful Moraga campus to celebrate in a carnival-like fashion Saint Mary's sesquicentennial. As their fancy dictated, participants could sample the fare of gourmet food trucks, purchase college apparel at a special booth, roll around in inflated bounce houses, attend academic presentations on everything from "Ancient Greek Astronomy" to "Confections of a Chocoholic," visit student exhibits, go on guided tours, sway to the music of a jazz band at a stage in front of the chapel and, most popular of all, ride on a seven-story-tall Ferris wheel.

With its 150-year anniversary celebrations now behind it, Saint Mary's is moving into an uncertain future. Only a handful of brothers are still teaching, and the president is no longer a religious. The college is banking on three traditions—Catholicism, the liberal arts and Lasallianism—to maintain its identity in the coming years. However, in his now classic study of the demise of religious colleges and universities, Father James Tunstead Burtchaell concludes that these three central purposes "have all been reinterpreted in such a way" in recent years that they no longer retain "much meaning." Take Lasallianism as an example. Given the economic realities of higher education, it is impossible any longer to define this tradition in terms of teaching the "just plain moneyless poor." The Christian Brothers once conducted gratuitous schools, but today the combined fees of Saint Mary's are about $50,000 a year. As a result, college officials have been reduced to defining Lasallianism as "student-centered" education. But what faith-based institution or secular college or university worth its salt does not aspire to that ideal? In fact, Lasallianism is often used as a mantra or talisman that "dissipates" energy rather than "focusing" it. Earlier we noted that the term was employed to deplore academic freedom and the dropping of football, as well as to support the education of adult learners. It has been invoked in so many different and sometimes contradictory ways that a respected faculty member was once moved to ask, "What does Lasallianism mean this year?" As a consequence, Burtchaell believes that Saint Mary's "is committed to a tradition so undefinable that it could never be violated."[308] Is he right? The future will tell.

Notes

CHAPTER 1

1. General biographical information on Alemany is taken from McGloin, *California's First Archbishop*.
2. Quoted in McGloin, *California's First Archbishop*, 25.
3. McKevitt, *University of Santa Clara*, 75–77.
4. Letter of August 25, 1862, copy, AASF.
5. McKevitt, *University of Santa Clara*, 77, 348, ft.33.
6. *San Francisco Daily Herald*, "Catholic College in California," March 31, 1860.
7. McDevitt, *Saint Mary's College*, 11.
8. List of Subscriptions for San Francisco College, 1859–1860, AASF.
9. Brother Cyril Ashe, "History of Saint Mary's College, 1863–1917," typed ms., 5, ASFD.
10. Quoted in McDevitt, *Saint Mary's College*, 27.
11. San Francisco: Valentine and Company, 1862, 29, ABLB.
12. Ashe, "History of SMC," 21.
13. Cash Book, September 22, 1862–December 31, 1869, AASF.
14. Alemany to George H. Briard, May 25, 1863, in Journal of Correspondence, August 14, 1862–May 7, 1868, 31, AASF.
15. Journal of Correspondence, August 14, 1862–May 7, 1868, 42, AASF.
16. Letter of July 31, 1863, Journal of Correspondence, August 14, 1862 May 7, 1868, 44, AASF.
17. John Paul Cosgrave to Brother Cyril Ashe, December 27, 1911. Quoted in McDevitt, *Saint Mary's College*, 37.

18. A letter of Brother Brindolin Finglas, FSC, Dublin, October 31, 1960, states that Father Grey's grandniece, Ms. Mary Hunston, believed that her granduncle amassed a fortune buying and selling real estate in San Francisco. Brother Matthew's citation. See ft. 55, ch. 2. I have not been able to find this letter among Brother Matthew's papers in ASMC.

19. Letter of January 8, 1864, Journal of Correspondence, August 14, 1862–May 7, 1868, 69, AASF.

20. Ashe, "History of SMC" 10.

21. Letter of September 23, 1864, Journal of Correspondence, August 14, 1862–May 7, 1868, 103, AASF.

22. Quoted in Ashe, "History of SMC," 13.

23. Letter of July 1865, copy, ASFD.

24. Ashe, "History of SMC," 12.

25. *San Francisco Directory*, 1862, 9.

CHAPTER 2

26. Letter of May 4, 1857, ACBR.

27. Letter of January 19, 1858, Journal of Correspondence, August 14, 1862–May 7, 1868, 61, AASF.

28. Letter of March 27, 1858, ACBR.

29. Alemany to Bartholomew Woodlock, June 15, 1858, copy, AASF.

30. Cardinal Barnabo to Brother Philippe, July 11, 1867, ACBR.

31. Note in French on the back of Cardinal Barnabo's letter, circa summer 1867, ACBR.

32. Brother Facile to Brother Patrick, May 24, 1868, quoted in "Latin in the United States, Memoir of Brother Assistant Reticius Gonnet," (1907), handwritten ms., 25–26, 205, ACBR.

33. Typed excerpt from the *New York Tablet*, July 16, 1868, ASFD.

34. Quoted in Cashin, *Christian Brothers*, 454–55.

35. Sam Roberts, "The Mayor is Shot," http://NYTimes.com/cityroom. blogs/the-mayor-is-shot.

36. Ashe, "History of SMC," 21–22.

37. Gloria Eive, "The Bells of Saint Mary's College," typed ms., 2012, 2.

38. Ashe, "History of SMC," 21.

39. "Destruction of Property in Various Parts of the City," October 22, 1868, http://sfmuseum.org/hist1 /1868 eq.html.

40. Anonymous, "District of San Francisco," n.d., typed, three-page ms., 1, ACBR.

41. Brother Justin to Brother Irlide Cazaneuve, February 1, 1876, ACBR.

42. "St. Mary's College Semi-Annual Examination," clipping, ACBR.

43. Rudolph, *Curriculum*, 44.

44. Ashe, "History of SMC," 39.
45. Letter of August 7, 1871, ACBR.
46. *History of California*, I, 43m, ABLB.
47. George W. Poultney to Brother Dennis Goodman, June 12, 1968; Poultney to Brother Dennis, September 5, 1968; notes of interview by Brother Matthew of George W. Poultney, n.d.; George W. Poultney, interviewed by Brother Cormac Murphy, October 30, 1968; Poultney to Brother Henry DeGroote, October 16, 1965; Brother Leo Meehan, "Outlooks and Insights," *Saint Mary's Collegian*, March 24, 1933, ASMC.
48. Ashe, "History of SMC," 23.
49. Bean and Rawls, *California*, 216.
50. See ft. 25.
51. "Forget 9-9-9: Here's a Simple Plan: 1," *New York Times*, October 16, 2011.
52. Ashe, "History of SMC," 5.
53. "St Mary's College, San Francisco, Cal., Conducted by the Christian Brothers," 1868, ASFD.
54. McDevitt, *Saint Mary's College*, 223.
55. Jackson Alpheus Graves to a Brother at Saint Mary's, circa 1911–12, ASMC.
56. Quoted in Zingg, *Harry Hooper*, 48. Zingg, who is the president of California State University–Chico, was once the dean of the School of Liberal Arts at Saint Mary's.
57. Ashe, "History of SMC," 21.
58. Zingg, *Harry Hooper*, 53.
59. "St. Mary's College, San Francisco, Cal., Conducted by the Christian Brothers," 1868, ASFD.
60. Graves, *Seventy Years in California*, 50–51, 53–54.

CHAPTER 3

61. Brother Justin to Brother Irlide, February 1, 1876, ACBR.
62. For a complete and critical historical treatment of the Latin Question, see Battersby, *History of the Institute, 1900–1925*. I would like to acknowledge my considerable debt to Battersby's excellent study for much of the factual material on the Latin Question found in this and succeeding chapters, although I have also done extensive original research on the topic and published three articles on it.
63. See Ronald Isetti, "Memorandum on the Habit," 149–91, especially 183, in Isetti and Loes, *Rule and Foundational Documents*. The volume was edited by the author and Brother Augustine Loes, FSC. Battersby offers

this alternative translation: "Those who compose this community are all laymen, without classical studies and of little culture."

64. "Rule of 1718," in Isetti and Loes, *Rule and Foundational Documents*, 96.

65. For a full treatment of the European historical development of the institute, see Battersby, *History of the Brothers, 1719–1798* and *History of the Institute, 1800–1850*.

66. "Notes of the late Brother Justin and Brother Maurelian [Sheel]," n.d., ACBR.

67. *San Francisco Monitor,* "The Christian Brothers in California," August 15, 1868, AASF.

68. "A Summary Account of the Introduction of Latin in the United States," handwritten brief prepared sometime in 1894, 3, ACBR.

69. Alemany to Brother Justin, March 12, 1879, ACBR.

70. Alemany to Brother Irlide, April 24, 1879, ACBR.

71. Brother Justin to Brother Irlide, June 23, 1879, ACBR.

72. Alemany to Brother Irlide, January 5, 1880, ACBR.

73. Brother Justin to Brother Patrick, February 11, 1880, ACBR.

74. Alemany to Brother Irlide, April 6, 1880, ACBR.

75. Letter of April 4, 1879, ACBR.

76. Graves, *My Seventy Years*, 50.

77. Ashe, "History of SMC," 23, 42.

78. McDevitt, *Saint Mary's College*, 94.

CHAPTER 4

79. Brother Jasper Fitzsimmons, "History of the District of San Francisco," typed ms., n.d., 2, ASFD.

80. Page 6, ASMC.

81. Brother Jasper, "History of the San Francisco District, Christian Brothers," n.d., typed ms., 2, ASFD.

82. Brother Joseph to my dear George, n .d., ASMC.

83. Ibid.

84. For a scholarly biography, see Lynn M. Hudson, *The Making of "Mammy" Pleasant: A Black Entrepreneur in Nineteenth-Century San Francisco* (Champaign: University of Illinois Press, 2002); see also "Pleasant's Story," http://mepleasant.com/story.html; "Mary Ellen Pleasant," http://answers.com/topic/ mary_ellen_pleasant.

85. Quoted in Ashe, "History of SMC," 62.

86. Brother Joseph to my dear George, n.d., ca. 1920s.

87. Catalogue of 1896–1897, 11, 39, ASMC.

88. *Oakland Tribune,* "Knave" clipping, November 1947[?], ASFD; *Oakland Tribune,* "Knave," September 22, 1968, 17cm, 20cm; Ashe, "History of

SMC," 91–92; McDevitt, *Saint Mary's College*, 114; *San Francisco Chronicle*, "A College in Ashes," clipping, September 24, 1894, ACBR; Brother Erminold to Brother Clementian Muth, October 12, 1894, ACBR.

89. Brother Genebern Steiner to Brother Clementian, May 15, 1895. ACBR.

90. Ibid.

91. Catalogue of 1896–1897, 20–21.

92. "Letter to Editor," quoted in McDevitt, *Saint Mary's College*, 125.

93. Quoted in Battersby, *History of Christian Brothers, 1900–1925*, 46.

94. Letter of May 18, 1898, quoted in Battersby, *History of Christian Brothers, 1900–1925*, 112.

95. "Circular Letter to Our Dear Brothers of the Districts of the United States," Administrative Circular No. 81, February 19, 1898 (Paris, 1898), 21, LSRL.

96. The results from the San Francisco District were recorded on four handwritten sheets of paper that can be found in the APGR. Bishop Byrne was able obtain eighty-four signatures from the San Francisco District.

97. Copy of the oath in ACBR.

98. "Decision about the Teaching of Latin," Administrative Circular No. 91, January 18, 1900 (Paris, 1900), 6, ACBR.

Chapter 5

99. Letter of May 23, 1900, quoted in Battersby, *History of the Christian Brothers, 1900–1925*, 202.

100. George W. Poultney, interviewed by Brother Cormac Murphy, October 30, 1968, ASMC.

101. Gregory Leggio, SJ, "Diary, 1906," Leggio Papers, Oregon Province Jesuit Archives, Gonzaga University, Spokane, Oregon. I am grateful to Gerald McKevitt, SJ, for supplying me with this source.

102. "College Items," October 1911, ASMC.

103. Zingg, *Harry Hooper*, 50.

104. Andrada, *They Did It Everytime*, 21.

105. McDevitt, *Saint Mary's College*, 162.

106. Anonymous, "A Brief History of Saint Mary's College," n.d., typed ms., 11, ACBR.

107. "Brother Alfred Brousseau Speaks of Brother Leo Meehan," *Brothers Speak of Leo Meehan* (Moraga, CA: Provincial Publications, November 1983), 17, 62–63.

108. Brother Cornelius Braeg, "Brother 'White' Leo, Part II," *Brickpile Seniors' Newsletter* (October 15, 1953), 3, ASMC.

109. Ibid.

110. *Oakland Tribune*, "Knave," September 22, 1968, 20cm; Battersby, *History of*

the Christian Brothers, 1900–1925, 613; Ashe, "History of SMC," 108.

111. McDevitt, *Saint Mary's College*, 167.

112. Brother Gregory to Catholic Friends, August 5, 1918, ASFD.

113. *Saint Mary's Men in the Great War* (Oakland, 1919), 5, ASFD.

114. Cardinal Gasparri to Brother Imier Lafabregue, April 15, 1923, in French, APGR. Emphasis added.

115. Burtchaell, *Dying of the Light*, 674. Emphasis added.

CHAPTER 6

116. Jack James, "Found—A Man Who Finds Sport Page Does a College a Whole Lot of Good," clipping, *San Francisco Examiner*, ca. 1921, ASMC.

117. "Lives–[Brother] Urban Gregory II," 7, ASFD. More likely, his salary was $1,200.

118. Andrada, *They Did It Everytime*, 30–57; McKevitt, *University of Santa Clara*, 189–93.

119. Andrada, *They Did It Everytime*, 63–65.

120. Ibid., 64–65.

121. Page 80. Copy in ASMC.

122. This scenario is spun out by John Biggins in "'The University that Never Was': The Untold Story of Why Saint Mary's Moved to Moraga rather than San Leandro," n.d., typed ms., 10, ASMC. It was written for a History Department pro-seminar conducted by the author.

123. Brother Joseph to Brother Abban Philip, March 29, 1927, ACBR.

124. Ibid., March 24, 1937, ACBR.

125. Brother Joseph to Victor Gerard and W. Harrison, March 21, 1926, AASF.

126. Quoted in "50 Years–Pride and Progress in Moraga," *Saint Mary's College News* 6, no. 1 (May 1977): 1, ASMC.

127. Brother Josephus, "Lives–[Brother] Urban Gregory II," 12; Brother Josephus, "Deceased Brothers of the District of San Francisco," n.d., typed ms., ASFD.

128. McDevitt, *Saint Mary's College*, 185.

129. Brother Josephus, "Lives–[B]rother Urban Gregory II," 2.

130. Brother Joseph to Brother Abban Philip, February 24, 1927, and March 29, 1927.

131. Brother Josephus, "Lives–[B]rother Urban Gregory II," 12.

132. McDevitt, *Saint Mary's College*, 185.

133. Brother Joseph to Brother Abban Philip, March 29, 1927.

134. McDevitt, *Saint Mary's College*, 190.

135. Brother Joseph to Brother Abban Philip, February 24, 1927.

136. James S. Dean, "Saint Mary's College, California," *Architect and*

Engineer LCVIII, no. 3 (September 1929): 35.

137. Quoted in Joy L. Choate, "A Place to Learn and Live," *Saint Mary's College Update* 17, no. 8 (Summer 1996): 8–9.

138. "Superintendent Granted Leave for Long Tour," February 1, 1929, ASMC.

139. Fenlon to my dear Brothers, ca. August 21, 1931

140. One-page photocopy of a tribute to Brother Joseph, with an accompanying photograph, taken from the school yearbook of 1928, ASMC.

CHAPTER 7

141. "Charles R. Schelfin Speaks of Brother Leo Meehan," in *The Alumni Speak of Brother Leo* (Moraga, CA: Archives Publications: April 1983), 51.

142. Bob McAndrews, "Alumnus Remembers Being in the First Graduating Class on the Moraga Campus," *Saint Mary's College Update* 19, no. 4 (Spring 1998): 4, 15, ASMC.

143. "Edward C. Massa Speaks of Brother Leo Meehan," in *Alumni Speak*, 18.

144. "Edward D. Cone Speaks of Brother Leo Meehan," in *Alumni Speak*, 43.

145. "Brother Dennis Goodman Speaks of Brother Leo Meehan," in *Brothers Speak*, 71. Brother Dennis's essay on Brother Leo is especially rich and insightful; much of the general biographical material on him is taken from this source.

146. Typed reviews of scholars designated as A, B, C, D, ACBR.

147. Meehan, *Living Upstairs*, 242.

148. "Charles R. Scheflin Speaks of Brother Leo Meehan," in *Alumni Speak*, 53.

149. "In the Beginning," 1, no. 1 (Spring 1931): 3, ASMC.

150. College Catalogue of 1928–1931, ASMC, 63–64.

151. "W. Edwin Swallow Speaks of Brother Leo Meehan," *Alumni Speak*, 16.

152. Andrada, *They Did It Everytime*, 10, 75–112.

153. Ibid, 78–91.

154. Ibid., 50–51, 73, 75–112, 129–32.

155. Ibid., 1, 65, 93, 96–98.

156. Ibid., 117, 119.

157. McKevitt, *University of Santa Clara*, 239–43, 250–52.

158. Ibid., 250–52.

159. McDevitt, *Saint Mary's College*, 203.

160. "Charles R. Scheflin Speaks of Brother Leo Meehan," in *Alumni Speak*, 52–53.

161. Quoted in Andrada, *They Did It Everytime*, 115.

162. Meehan, *Temple of the Spirit*, 66–67. Although written many years after Brother Leo's time as chancellor, these thoughts most likely expressed his

attitude toward intercollegiate athletics in earlier years.

163. Leonard Thomas to Hagerty, March 15, 1933, ASMC.

164. "Edward D. Cone Speaks of Brother Leo," in *Alumni Speak*, 43.

CHAPTER 8

165. Brother Alfred Brousseau, "Some Thoughts on Brother Albert Rahill," n.d., typed ms., 15; Brother Alfred Brousseau, "Brother Albert Rahill," one-page typed biography, ASFD.

166. "Saint Mary's Prexy Prefers Chemistry," unidentified New York newspaper clipping, November 6, 1935, ASFD.

167. *Time*, "Education: Saint Mary's Auction," August 2, 1937; McDevitt, *Saint Mary's College*, 219.

168. Letter in AASF.

169. *Saint Mary's Collegian*, "Archbishop Mitty Buys Saint Mary's College for $715,000," September 17, 1937, ASMC.

170. "Diamond Jubilee of Saint Mary's College," *Moraga Quarterly* 8, no. 5 (Summer 1938): 210, ASMC.

171. Ibid., 211, no. 23 (December 3, 1938), 74.

172. *Oakland Tribune*, "Telegram Tells 'Slip' Madigan That He's Fired," March 12, 1940.

173. Art Cohn, "I Was Fired Because of Feud: Madigan," *Oakland Tribune*, March 12, 1940.

174. *Oakland Tribune*, "Slip Charges Personal Feud," March 13, 1940.

175. "Saint Mary's Head Arrives to See Fordham Game," unidentified New York City newspaper clipping, November 6, 1935, ACBR.

176. Andrada, *They Did It Everytime*, 153.

177. Quoted in Andrada, *They Did It Everytime* 155.

178. Brousseau, "Brother Albert Rahill."

179. Andrada, *They Did It Everytime,* 131–32.

180. Brother Mel to the author, May 8, 2010.

CHAPTER 9

181. Stanley Gilliam to Brother Brendan Kneale, June 5, 1974, ASFD.

182. "Popular SM Teachers Leave School," ASMC.

183. According to Brother Dennis, Brother John Hoffman, president of Mont La Salle Vineyards, came up with this estimate. See "Brother Dennis Goodman Speaks of Brother Leo Meehan," in *Brothers Speak*, 72. See also, "Brother Alfred Brousseau Speaks of Brother Leo," in *Brothers Speak*, 44. Brother Alfred does careful calculations of Brother

Leo's probable income.

184. *Wisconsin State Journal* (Madison), "Monk to Renounce Vows After 40 Years in Order," October 29, 1941.

185. "On Knowing When to Quit," reproduced in *Brothers Speak*, 9–11 of the appendix.

186. See the files of APGR in Rome.

187. Brother Josephus Mangan, "Confidential Report," ca. early 1941, 6–7, AASF.

188. Approximately one hundred former students sent Brother Alfred their recollections of Brother Leo, and nearly all of them are extremely, almost worshipfully, positive.

189. Clipping of February 27, 1942, ASMC.

190. "Response by Brother Cornelius to mimeographed SUMMARY OF NEW PROGRAM of College studies issued Sept. 1943 by the head of the Administration of Saint Mary's College, California," typed ms., ca. November 1943, 1–5; see also Brother Cornelius, "Disadvantages of the Present (Fall 1944) St. Mary's Study Plan," typed ms., 2, ASMC.

191. "Response by Brother Cornelius…," 1.

192. Andrada, *They Did It Everytime*, 169–76.

193. Ibid., 180.

194. Letter of February 26, 1945, AASF.

CHAPTER 10

195. Brother Thomas Levi, interview by Brother Hilary Latour for the Brothers Oral History Project, July, 1992, 34, ASFD.

196. Ibid., 34–35.

197. Letter of November 19, 1950, ASFD.

198. Andrada, *They Did It Everytime*, 215–21.

199. "Future of St. Mary's College," working paper, December 7, 1951, ASFD.

200. Agenda for Visitor's Council Meeting, November 7, 1953, ASFD.

201. Brother Jasper to Archbishop Mitty, September 6, 1942, AASF.

202. Minutes of the Visitor's Council Meeting, November 17, 1951, ASFD.

203. "A Financial Analysis of the District," March 8, 1955, ASFD.

204. Information supplied by provincial archivist Andrea Miller in an e-mail to the author on August 22, 2008.

205. Archbishop Mitty to Andrew Burke, July 2, 1956, AASF.

206. Brother Brendan Kneale, "Brother Thomas Levi (1916–2004)," necrological notice, October 14, 2004, 7, ASFD.

207. Brother Thomas oral interview, 39, 50–51.

208. Brother Thomas to Brother Alfred, May 26, 1953, ASFD.

209. "A Tribute to Dr. James L. Hagerty," *Congressional Record,* Proceedings and Debates of the 85th Congress, Second Session, August 4, 1958, 1–2.

210. "Convocation Address," *Saint Mary's College Educational Perspectives* 2, no. 2 (Spring 1985): 54.

211. Ibid., 54–55.

212. This is the title of a candid, hard-hitting article Brother Alfred wrote for the *Religious Educator* in March 1946, 97–99. In it, he asserted, "Still, it would seem that in some portions of the Institute and with certain Brothers, there remains a definite cult of ignorance, which is more of a clinging to form than an intelligent application of the principles of our Founder."

213. "General Directives," ca. 1957, ASFD.

CHAPTER 11

214. Brother Thomas oral interview, 67.

215. Brother Brendan Kneale, "Brother Sylvester Albert Plotz," necrological notice, January 29, 1962, 11, ASFD.

216. Brother Albert to Brother Jerome, January 16, 1962, ASFD.

217. Letter of June 21, 1957, ASFD.

218. Brother Albert to Archbishop Mitty, February 20, 1959, AASF.

219. "President's Report, 1959–1960," December 1959, ACBR.

220. Helen Marie Ciernick, "Student Life on Catholic-College Campuses in the San Francisco Bay Area during the 1960s," PhD diss., Catholic University of America, 2003, 78–82, 127–29.

221. "Brother Albert Plotz, F.S.C.," necrological notice, 20.

222. Brother Mel Anderson, "Eulogy for Brother Michael Quinn," Saint Mary's College, March 19, 2009, *Educational Horizons* 9, no. 1 (Fall/Winter 2009–10): 7.

223. "Brother Michael Appointed Saint Mary's President," news release, February 5, 1962; Brother Jerome to Director and Brothers, February 5, 1962, ASMC.

224. *The Liberal Arts: The Language of Free Men* (Moraga, CA: Saint Mary's College, 1963), 2, ASMC.

225. Excerpts from "Inaugural Address," *Gael* yearbook, 1963, 139, ASMC.

226. "Century II Program of Saint Mary's College: A Presentation of the Development Office," *Forum* 1, no. 5 (October 15, 1967): 27, ASFD.

227. *Day for a Dedication*, Century II pamphlet (Moraga, CA: Saint Mary's College, 1967), 2.

228. "Eulogy for Brother Michael," 6.

229. "The Movement Grows," ASMC.

230. *Saint Mary's Alumnus* 18, no. 1 (Summer 1969): 5–7, ASMC.

231. "Whitehurst Returns for Graduation Speech," May 17, 1978, ASMC.

CHAPTER 12

232. "Report of the Interpersonal Relations Committee," May 10–11, 1977, ASMC.

233. Anderson, *Years of Yearning*, 23.

234. Ibid., 131–32.

235. Ibid., 34.

236. Ibid., 139–42.

237. "Slakey Assumes Academic Reins," *Saint Mary's College News* 2, no. 3 (September 1971): 3, ASMC.

238. "Comments Sent to Brother Ronald Isetti by Brother Mel Anderson, FSC, on 'Saint Mary's College in the Seventies,'" September 20, 1978, 4.

239. Anderson, *Years of Yearning*, 1, 77.

240. "Report on the Site Visit to Saint Mary's College," October 15–17, 1975, 21, ASMC.

241. Anderson, *Years of Yearning*, 216.

242. "Report of the Interpersonal Relations Committee," 4, 5, 6, 9, 11, 13, ASMC.

243. Anderson, *Years of Yearning*, 234.

244. "Report of the WASC On-Site Visit," October 12–14, 1977, 43, ASMC.

245. Kay Anderson to Brother Mel, February 27, 1978, ASMC.

246. Anderson, *Years of Yearning*, 248–49.

247. Letter in ASMC.

248. "Report of the WASC Visit, March 12–14, 1980," 5, ASMC.

249. Anderson, *Years of Yearning*, 346.

250. Ibid.

CHAPTER 13

251. *Saint Mary's Collegian*, "College Unveils New President," February 20, 1997, ASMC.

252. "President's Self-Evaluation," November 8, 1999, 18.

253. Brother Craig to the author, October 19, 2012.

254. Keith Campbell e-mail to the Faculty, December 5, 1999, ASMC; see also "Responses to Open-Ended Questions of Full-Time Faculty Members," Academic Administrators Evaluation Committee, ca.

December 1999, 2, 6, 9, 14, 18, 23, 25, 29, 32, 33, 37, 82, 90, 92.

255. "Responses," 12, 27, 30, 35, 39, 40, 41, 46, 49, 50, 51, 52, 53, 54, 55, 56, 59, 60, 61, 62, 63, 65, 67, 87, 103, 105; Maureen Wesolowski e-mail to the Faculty, October 1, 1999.

256. Rebecca Carroll, "Senate Resolution: Regarding the Status of Staff," e-mail to Faculty, February 3, 2000, ASMC; see also, "Responses," 19.

257. Elizabeth Bell, "St. Mary's Students Protest," *San Francisco Chronicle*, clipping, November 23, 1999, ASMC.

258. Bill Jasper to the Board of Trustees, December 3, 1999.

259. "President's Self Evaluation," 7–8.

260. "Responses," 84. Others agreed; see pp. 3, 6, 10, 15, 77, 107, 108.

261. Quoted in Joseph Wakelee-Lynch, "Shake Up in Play, The New Vision for Gael Athletics is Taking Form," *Saint Mary's College Update* 25, no. 3 (Winter 2005): 20, ASMC.

262. Quoted in Ron Kroichick, "A Quiet Fall: Few Miss Football at St. Mary's," *San Francisco Chronicle*, clipping, November 14, 2004, ASMC.

263. Brother Stanislaus Campbell to the Saint Mary's Community, January 30, 2000, ASMC.

264. Brother Raphael e-mail to the author, September 16, 2010.

265. Carrie Sturrock, "Man, 84, Charged in Investment Scam," *San Francisco Chronicle*, clipping, January 20, 2005, ASMC.

266. Carrie Sturrock, "Walnut Creek Man Ordered to Pay Millions to Victim," *San Francisco Chronicle*, clipping, December 29, 2004, ASMC.

267. "Report by the Special Committee," 15.

268. Copy in ASMC.

269. "Report by the Special Committee," 2.

270. Ibid., 53.

271. Carrie Sturrock, "Decision to Go Ahead with Building Unusual," *San Francisco Chronicle*, clipping, September 7, 2004.

272. Dean E. Murphy, "112 Million Promised to College Turns Out to be All Promise and No Cash," newspaper clipping, September 26, 2004, ASMC.

273. Jackie Burrell and Stanley Donaldson, "St. Mary's President Steps Down," *Contra Costa Times*, clipping, September 22, 2004, ASMC.

274. Copy in ASMC; see also "President Resigns as College is Victimized in Pledge Scam," *Saint Mary's College Update* 25, no. 3 (Winter 2005): 2, ASMC.

275. Moore to the Saint Mary's College Community, September 21, 2004, ASMC.

276. Ibid., December 9, 2004, ASMC.

277. "Statement Expecting Formal Acknowledgment of Responsibility by Board of Trustees," October 7, 2004, ASMC.

278. Moore to Members of the Saint Mary's Community, October 15,

2004, ASMC.

279. "Franz a Man of Honor," clipping, September 23, 2004, ASMC.

280. Marginal comment on the ms., 2012.

281. Robert M. Figliulo to Saint Mary's University Community, December 20, 2006, ASMC.

282. Brother Ronald to the Saint Mary's Community, December 20, 2006, ASMC.

283. Matt Krupnick, "St. Mary's Reveals Ex-President, Student Had 'Sexual' Encounter," *Contra Costa Times*, clipping, December 21, 2006, ASMC.

284. Brother Craig, "Dedication Remarks—J.C. Gatehouse Hall," October 5, 2000, ASMC.

285. "Brother Craig Evaluation: Characteristic Phrases," Presidential Evaluation Committee, ca. 1999, 6.

Chapter 14

286. "Of Shepherds and Stewards: A Conversation with College Leaders," *Saint Mary's Magazine* 26, no. 3 (Spring 2006): 14–15, ASMC

287. "Embodying Our Traditions: The Inauguration of Brother Ronald Gallagher, FSC," *Saint Mary's Magazine* 26, no. 2 (Winter 2005): 19.

288. Erin Hallissy, "A Closer Look at Catholicism," *Saint Mary's Magazine* 27, no. 1 (Fall 2006): 1, 5, ASMC.

289. *San Francisco Business Times*, "Saint Mary's Cuts Longtime Extension Program," June 12, 2005, http:// bizjournals.com/eastbay/stories.

290. Brother Mel to the author, October 19, 2010.

291. "Comments to Brother Ronald…" 16.

292. Carl Guarneri e-mail to the author, October 3, 2012.

293. "Embodying Our Traditions," 1–17.

294. Tomas Gomez-Arias e-mail to Beth Dobkin, September 30, 2011, ASMC.

295. Randall Andrada e-mail to the author, December 27, 2011.

296. Carl Guarneri e-mail to Dear Colleagues, May 9, 2012; Steven Cortright e-mail to Guarneri, May 8, 2012. Guarneri's earlier e-mail is reproduced in the main in the later one.

297. Letter, "Dear Saint Mary's Donor," reproduced in the blog, http:// halfwaytoconcord.com/bill-ayers.

298. Message from the President," January 21, 2009, http://stmary's-ca. edu/about-smc/president/messages/item-display.html?ID=2040.

299. Wolff to President Gallagher, March 1, 2005, ASMC.

300. Ibid., February 27, 2008, ASMC.

301. "Report of the WASC Special Visit Team on October 20 to 30,

2009," 5, 12, 13, 17, 22, 23, ASMC.

302. Brother Ronald e-mail to Members of the Saint Mary's Community, March, 2013.

303. Ibid.

304. Andy Katz Blog, "Analyzing the Saint Mary's Sanctions," ESPN Men's Basketball, http://espn.go.com/men's-college-basketball.blog/-/name/katz-andy.

305. John Wilner, "Saint Mary's Basketball Punished by NCAA for Recruiting Violations," *Contra Costa Times*, March 1, 2013, http://contracostatimes.com/breaking-news.

306. Jeff Eisenberg, "Crippling NCAA Sanctions Jeopardize Saint Mary's Recent Run of Success," Yahoo sports, February 1, 2013, http://ca..sports.yahoo.com/blogs/ncaab-the-dagger/crippling-ncaa-sanctions-jeopardize-saint-mary's.

307. "A Special Announcement," e-mail to Saint Mary's faculty, March 26, 2013.

308. Burtchaell, *Dying of the Light*, 694, 701.

Bibliography

Anderson, Mel. *Years of Yearning: A Memoir by Brother Mel Anderson, FSC, President of Saint Mary's College, 1969–1997*. San Ramon, CA: Vision Press, 2011.

Andrada, Randall. *They Did It Everytime: The Saga of the Saint Mary's Gaels*. San Francisco, CA: Powder River Press, 1975.

Bancroft, Hubert Howe. *History of California, 1542–1880*. San Francisco, CA: The History Company, 1886.

Battersby, W.J. (Clair). *The History of the Brothers of the Christian Schools in the Eighteenth Century, 1719–1798*. London: Waldegrave, 1960.

————. *The History of the Institute of the Brothers of the Christian Schools in the Nineteenth Century, 1800–1850*. London: Waldegrave, 1961.

————. *The History of the Institute of the Brothers of the Christian Schools: The Brothers in the United States, 1900–1925*. Winona, MN: St. Mary's College Press, 1967.

Bean, Walton, and James W. Rawls. *California: An Interpretive History*. 8th ed. Boston: McGraw-Hill, 2003.

Burtchaell, James Tunstead. *The Dying of the Light: The Disengagement of Colleges and Universities from Their Christian Churches*. Grand Rapids, MI: Eerdmans Publishing, 1998.

Cashin, Angelus Gabriel. *The Christian Brothers in the United States, 1848–1948: A Century of Catholic Education*. New York: Declan N. McMullen, 1948.

Ciernick, Helen Marie. "Student Life on Catholic-College Campuses in the San Francisco Bay Are in the 1960s." PhD diss. Catholic University of America, Washington, D.C., 2003.

Graves, J.A. *My Seventy Years in California, 1857–1927.* Los Angeles: Times-Mirror Press, 1927.

Isetti, Ronald, and Augustine Loes. *Rule and Foundational Documents: John Baptist de La Salle.* Landover, MD: Lasallian Publications, 2002.

McDevitt, Matthew. *The First Century of St. Mary's College (1863–1963)* Moraga, CA: Saint Mary's College, 1963.

McGloin, John B. *California's First Archbishop: The Life of Joseph Sadoc Alemany, O.P., 1814–1888.* New York: Herder and Herder, 1966.

McKevitt, Gerald. *The University of Santa Clara: A History, 1851–1977.* Stanford, CA: Stanford University Press, 1979.

Meehan, Francis. *Living Upstairs: Reading for Profit and Pleasure.* New York: E.P. Dutton, 1942.

———. *The Temple of the Spirit: A Pathway to Personal Peace.* New York: E.P. Dutton, 1948.

Rudolph, Frederick. *Curriculum: A History of the American Undergraduate Course of Study Since 1636.* San Francisco, CA: Jossey-Bass, 1977.

Zingg, Paul. *Harry Hooper: An American Baseball Life.* Chicago: University of Illinois Press, 1993.

Index

A

academic senate 157, 159, 171, 177, 178, 179
Accolti, Father Michael 13
Alemany, Archbishop Joseph Sadoc 11–20, 22, 23–24, 25, 27–28, 30–31, 38–39, 41–46, 48–49, 132
Aloia, Gregory 140
American Protective Association 54
Anderson, Brother Mel 9, 109, 145–146, 147, 149–157, 159–163, 169, 176
Anderson, Dr. Kay 156
Andrada, Randall 10, 64, 76–77, 94, 96, 98, 119–120
Ashe, Brother Cyril 10, 29, 34, 46
Athletic Review Task Force 168

B

Banker, John Slade 166, 169
Barnabo, Cardinal Alessandro 24
basketball walkout 153
Beatie, Brother William 156–158, 160, 178

Bedford, Clay 140
Bennett, Randy 182
Black Friday 102
Board of Athletic Control 104
Board of Regents 126, 169
Board of Trustees 126, 146, 149, 153, 159, 160, 163, 165, 168, 170, 171, 172, 174, 176, 181, 184
Bogus Pledge Scandal 169
Braeg, Brother Cornelius 117, 118, 135
Bransiet, Brother Philippe 23–24, 55
Brennan, Brother David 160, 162
Brennan, Father Richard 20
Brigham Young University 149, 183
Brousseau, Brother Alfred 98, 100–101, 122–123, 125–127, 129–131, 171
Brown, Dean Thomas 153, 159
building projects 14, 15, 16, 44, 48, 69, 78, 81, 136, 138, 139, 146, 152, 167, 170
Butler, James Everett 102
Byrne, Bishop Thomas Sebastian 56, 57

C

Campbell, Brother Stanislaus 169
Cardwell, Brother Kenneth 9
Cassin, Brendan "B.J." 160
Catholic University of America
    (Washington, D.C.) 10, 66, 88,
    103, 130, 154
Century II Campaign 137–139
Chan, Dr. Lionel 170
chapel occupation 153
Christian Brothers College (Saint
    Louis) 58
Christian Brothers High School
    (Sacramento) 80
Colbrandt, Conrad 166, 167, 169, 170
Coleman, Brother Bertram 145
Congregation of the Propagation of
    the Faith (*Propaganda Fide*) 24,
    56–58
Cortright, Professor Steven 179
Croke, Father James 13, 14, 16, 21, 25
Crowley, Brother Austin 110–113, 116,
    120–122, 127
Curran, Brother Calixtus 69
Curran, Brother Jack 163

D

Dean Witter Company 81
De La Salle, Saint John Baptist 39, 81,
    88, 103, 128
Devine, Dr. James 163
Devlin, Dr. Keith 170
Diamond Anniversary Celebration 103
Dobkin, Provost Bethami "Beth" 10,
    177, 180, 182
Dominicans 11, 42, 49, 140
Donahue, Dr. James A. 184
Donovan, John J. 83, 146
Dooley, Brother Albian Benedict 60
Downey, Brother Sabinian 25, 28
Doyle, Brother Florinus Peter 60

E

evening law school 61, 77, 88

F

Fenlon, Brother Joseph 48, 73, 78, 81,
    83–84, 147
fire of 1894 52
fire of 1918 59
Fitzpatrick, Brother Gustavus 28
Flanagan, Dennis 142
Fordham University (New York) 94,
    102, 107
Franz, Brother Craig 9, 160, 162–171,
    173, 174, 180

G

Gallagher, Brother Ronald 172, 174,
    176–180, 182–184
Gallagher, Father Cornelius 19
Gasparri, Cardinal Pietro 71, 128
Gaynor, William J. (Brother Adrian
    Denys) 25, 27
General Chapter of 1923 71, 128
George, Henry 33
Giurlanda, Dr. Paul 175
Gleeson, Father William 32, 36, 37
Golden Jubilee Celebrations 64
Goto, Kazuo 146
Graves, Jackson Alpheus 31, 36, 41, 46
Great Books Program 50, 116–118,
    121, 127–128
Great San Francisco Earthquake
    (1868) 30
Grey, Father Peter J. 19, 20, 21, 45
Griffin, Brother Cianan 25, 28
Guarneri, Dr. Carl 10, 179
Guilday, Monsignor Peter 103

H

Hagerty, Dr. James L. 90, 98, 116,
    127–128
Hanna, Archbishop Edward J. 69, 81,
    86, 97
Harlow, Jean 109
Harrington, Father John F. 16, 18, 19, 20
Hibernia Savings and Loan Bank (Bank
    of Hibernia) 14, 43

Higgins, Brother Dimidrian 25, 28
History of the Catholic Church in
California 32
Holy Names College (Oakland) 69
Hooper, Harry 62
Hoover, President Herbert 77, 94
Hutchins, Robert Maynard 104, 105,
118, 155
Hyde, Dr. Monica 158
Hynes, Dr. William J. 10, 158–160, 165

I

Institute for Professional Development
(IPD) 155, 156, 157
Integrated Liberal Arts Program (Integral
Program) 127–129, 177
International Institute of Banking and
Finance 155
Interpersonal Relations ("Love")
Committee 155
Irvine, James 79, 159

J

"J.C. Gatehouse" (Brousseau) Hall
166–167
Jesuits (Society of Jesus) 12, 13, 39, 40,
44, 45, 55, 60, 97, 106
Johnson, John Henry 124
Johnson, President Lyndon Baines 137
Joy, Brother Xavier 132, 139

K

Kane, Brother Benezet Thomas 32
Keith, William 118
Kent State Protest 150
King, Lieutenant Commander Clyde
114

L

Larkin, Ray 174
La Salle High School (Pasadena) 149
La Salle University (Philadelphia)
61, 163

Latin Question, the 9, 39, 55–58, 67,
71–72, 118, 130
Lawrence, Ernest Orlando 101
"League of the Cross" Cadet Corps 54
Leggio, Father Gregory 60
Lemke-Santangelo, Dr. Gretchen 10
Leo, Pope, XIII 49, 58, 89
Levi, Brother Thomas 122–128,
131–132
Loubet, Brother Nicet-Joseph 129, 130
Loyola University of Chicago 136
Lyons, Father James 97

M

Madigan, Edward Patrick "Slip" 73,
75–77, 93–97, 102–107, 109,
112, 140, 142
Mallon, Brother Gregory 60, 67, 69,
75, 77–78, 80–82
Mangan, Brother Josephus 75, 79, 80
Manhattan College (New York) 26, 45,
59, 128
Maritain, Jacques 128–129
Master's in Contemporary Theology 134
Maynard, Gwin 37
McCann, Brother Agnon 62, 92
McDevitt, Brother Matthew 10, 13,
46, 64, 69, 80, 98
McKevitt, Father Gerald 97
McKinnon, Brother Leo 66
McLeod, Dean William 152, 160
McMahon, Brother Bettelin 47, 48,
52, 58
Meehan, Brother Leo 66, 86–89, 91,
96–98, 111
Meehan, DeNeze Brown 112
Melody, Brother Vivian 80
Miles, John 135
Miller, Congressman George P. 128, 141
Mitty, Archbishop John J. 100, 102–
103, 111, 113, 121, 124, 126,
132–133
Moller, Brother Pirmian 25, 28
Mont La Salle Vineyards 126

Moore, Nicholas 169, 171
Moraga Development Company 79
Moraga Manifesto 142
Moraga Quarterly 90, 91, 98, 128
Murphy, Brother Mark 160
Murphy, Brother Patrick 25–26, 32, 44–45
Murphy, J. Philip 104

N

National Collegiate Athletic Association (NCAA) 182–184
Navy Pre-Flight School 112–116
NCAA sanctions 183
Notre Dame University 75, 76, 93, 107, 137

O

Oblates of Mary Immaculate 45
O'Connor, Brother Felix 58
Odell Johnson Affair, the 151–153
O'Donnell, Brother Erminold 52
O'Melia (O'Malley), Brother Walter 54
open house demonstration 153
Oppenheimer, J. Robert 101

P

Parmisano, Father Stanley 128
Patton, Brother Raphael 9, 169
Pellerin, Brother Fabrician 60–62, 64, 66, 71
Petermann, Brother Emilian 25, 28, 37
Philosophy 1a 91
Phoenix baseball team 64
phone booth stuffing 135
Pius, Pope, IX 11, 15, 24
Pius, Pope, XI 71
Pleasant, Mary Ellen 48, 190
Plotz, Brother Albert 131–132, 135, 140
Pollock, Dr. Rafael Alan 137, 140, 142, 150
Porcella, Dr. Edward 9
Progress and Poverty 33
public academies 90, 91

Purcell, Bishop John Baptist 12

Q

Quinn, Brother Michael 131, 133, 135–137, 145
Quinn, Father William 25

R

Rabut, Brother Facile 23–26
Rahill, Brother Albert 99, 100–103, 105, 108–110
Reagan, Governor Ronald 132
Report by the Special Committee Regarding the Failed Anonymous Pledges (Cooley-Godward Report) 170
Ribeyron, Jean M. 91
Riordan, Archbishop William P. 48, 49, 52, 56, 58, 60, 69
Rodriquez-Paneda, Brother Julius 135
Roper (Larson), Dr. Katherine 9
Rosenberg Foundation 127
Roxby, Dr. Robert 9, 156, 176
Ruegg, Brother Dominic 153–156, 164, 176

S

Saint Francis Hotel (San Francisco) 69
Saint John's College (Annapolis) 117, 177
Saint John's College (Santa Fe) 154
Saint John's College (Washington, D.C.) 61
Saint Joseph's Academy (Oakland) 43, 77
Saint Mary's Club 96
Saint Mary's College High School (Berkeley) 77, 82, 99, 113
Saint Mary's Park 15
Saint Mary's University (Winona) 162, 172
Sanderl, Brother Michael 175
San Francisco Earthquake (1906) 59
Sanguine Tuesday 142
San Leandro campus 78, 79, 80, 81, 82, 102, 192
Santa Clara University (Santa Clara

College) 12–13, 31, 51, 64, 96–97, 106–107, 149, 152, 184
Savio, Mario 144
Schimelfenig, Marianne 163
School of Arts and Letters (Liberal Arts) 159
School of Education 60
School of Engineering 60, 89
School of Extended Education (SEED) 176
School of Science 108, 166, 170
Schorcht, Frederick 34, 35
Scudder, John W. 132
Servicemen's Readjustment Act of 1944 (G.I. Bill) 121
Sesquicentennial Celebration 185
Shaw, Lawrence T. "Buck" 106
Sheen, Monsignor Fulton J. 87
Simon, William G. "Bill" 98, 112
Slakey, Dr. Thomas 9, 150, 153–154, 178
Smith, Brother Robert 127
Sperling, Dr. John 156
Spirit of Saint Mary's Campaign 166
Spottiswood, Professor John 21
Stagg, Amos Alonzo 120
Stampp, Dr. Sara "Sally" 165, 168, 177
Stanford University 76–77
Steele, Captain George W. 114
Steiner, Brother Genebern 25, 28
Strader, Norman P. 104
Student Army Training Corps (SATC) 69–70
Student Protests 149, 165, 168
Students for Progressive Action Now (SPAN) 141–144, 147, 157, 179
Swope, Lieutenant Commander Gerard, Jr. 120

T

Taafe, Professor Lawrence 35
Thomas Aquinas College (Santa Paula) 177

Tracol Limited and Forefront Properties 166
Treacy, Brother Lewis 86
Trouble Along the Way (movie) 106
Trustee Presidential Evaluation Committee 169

U

Universal Saint Mary's Night 91
University of California, Berkeley 30, 51, 73, 75, 88, 111, 112
University of Chicago 104, 118, 158
University of Phoenix 155, 176
University of San Francisco (Saint Ignatius College) 12, 31, 60, 100, 135, 140, 149
University of Southern California 73, 98, 118
University of the Pacific (Stockton) 17, 119

W

Wedemeyer, Herman 119–120
Wensinger, Francis S. 48
West, Brother Jerome 136
Western Association of Schools and Colleges (WASC) 127, 134, 154, 155, 156, 157, 177, 179, 180, 181, 184
Western Training Center for the Federal Civil Defense Administration 125
Whitehurst, Daniel 10, 142–144
William Ayers controversy 180
Wolff, Ralph A. 180, 181

X

Xaverian Brothers 24

Z

Zellarbach, James David 127
Zingg, Dr. Paul 63, 159

About the Author

R onald Isetti attended the University
of the Pacific, where he earned
his bachelor's and master's degrees. His
doctorate in history is from the University
of California–Berkeley. For some thirty-
five years, he taught American, modern
Chinese and modern Japanese history at
Saint Mary's College of California. From
1960 to 1995, he was a member of the
Christian Brothers order. His earlier books
include a history of the Christian Brothers
on the West Coast and a biography of
the first American superior general. He
has also published articles on American
civil religion in history journals. Currently,
he lives in retirement in Palm Springs,
California, where he spends most of his
time walking, reading and writing.